SMALL LANGUAGE MODELS FOR BIG RESULTS: THE ROLE OF COMPACT AI IN MODERN APPLICATIONS

Rakesh Kumar

This book is dedicated to Lord Ganesha, the remover of obstacles, the god of wisdom, and the harbinger of success. In the world of technology and innovation, it is often said that the greatest breakthroughs come when we push past the challenges and barriers that seem insurmountable. In much the same way, Lord Ganesha, with his unique form and infinite wisdom, symbolizes the ability to overcome difficulties and achieve success, no matter the scale of the challenge. His presence is believed to guide us towards the right path, helping us navigate the complexities of life and work with grace and understanding.

As we embark on this exploration of small language models and compact AI, we seek inspiration from Lord Ganesha's qualities: his intellect, his problem-solving abilities, and his capacity to make things easier and more efficient. Just as Lord Ganesha is known for his creative ingenuity and innovative solutions, this book aims to unravel the potential of AI that can make complex processes simpler and more impactful.

In dedicating this work to Lord Ganesha, we acknowledge the divine guidance that inspires creativity, innovation, and the pursuit of knowledge. May his blessings pave the way for deeper understanding and success in our endeavors, helping us clear the path to new discoveries and advancements in technology.

CONTENTS

INTRODUCTION

In the rapidly evolving world of Artificial Intelligence (AI), language models have become the cornerstone of numerous breakthroughs across industries. From natural language processing to healthcare, finance, and customer service, AI-powered models are transforming how we interact with technology. However, as these models grow in size and complexity, the demand for more efficient, accessible, and scalable solutions has never been greater.

Enter small language models—compact, lightweight, and incredibly powerful. These models provide a novel approach to solving the challenges posed by large-scale AI systems, offering a sweet spot between performance and efficiency. With the advancement of techniques such as model compression, pruning, and distillation, small language models now deliver impressive results in a fraction of the time and computational cost compared to their larger counterparts.

In this book, Small Language Models for Big Results: The Role of Compact AI in Modern Applications, we will explore the growing significance of these smaller models in today's AI landscape. We will delve into the technical underpinnings that make small language models both powerful and efficient, the methods used to train and optimize them, and the diverse applications that are benefiting from their use. From enhancing customer experiences in real-time applications to enabling healthcare innovations and driving sustainability, compact AI models are not just a trend—they represent the future of practical AI.

Whether you are a data scientist, AI enthusiast, or business leader looking to harness the power of AI in a cost-effective and scalable manner, this book provides valuable insights and hands-on examples. We will cover the potential and limitations of small models, show how they are being applied across industries, and discuss their role in democratizing AI by making cutting-edge technology more accessible to a wider audience.

By the end of this journey, you will not only understand the transformative power of small language models but also gain a deeper appreciation of their potential to deliver big results—faster, smarter, and more efficiently. Join us as we explore how compact AI is shaping the future of technology, one model at a time.

THE SHIFT TOWARD COMPACT AI

As artificial intelligence (AI) has evolved, the demand for increasingly powerful models has driven the development of large, sophisticated language models. These models, such as GPT-3 and BERT, have demonstrated remarkable capabilities in natural language understanding and generation. However, their size, computational requirements, and energy consumption pose significant challenges, including:

- **High Costs**: Training and deploying large models require substantial financial and hardware investments.
- **Accessibility Barriers**: Smaller organizations and researchers often lack the resources to leverage such models effectively.
- **Environmental Impact**: The carbon footprint associated with training and maintaining large AI models is a growing concern.

Why Compact AI?

Compact AI, characterized by smaller, more efficient language models, addresses these challenges by focusing on:

1. **Efficiency**: Compact models are designed to achieve similar performance levels as their larger counterparts while using fewer resources.
2. **Scalability**: Smaller models can be deployed on edge devices, smartphones, and IoT systems, enabling AI

to reach broader and more diverse audiences.

3. **Accessibility**: Reduced computational demands lower the entry barrier for researchers, startups, and developers in emerging economies.
4. **Sustainability**: By consuming less energy, compact models contribute to reducing the environmental impact of AI.

Key Innovations Enabling Compact AI

- **Model Compression**: Techniques such as pruning, quantization, and knowledge distillation allow large models to be reduced in size without significant performance loss.
- **Specialized Architectures**: Advances like transformers optimized for low-resource environments enable efficient processing while maintaining output quality.
- **Hardware Synergy**: Collaboration between AI developers and hardware manufacturers has resulted in chips and processors tailored to compact model execution.

Real-World Impact

The shift toward compact AI is already revolutionizing industries:

- **Healthcare**: Compact models power diagnostics and patient support systems in resource-constrained settings.
- **Education**: AI tutors and language tools are now accessible via mobile devices, bridging gaps in underserved communities.
- **Business**: Lightweight AI solutions enable cost-effective customer service automation and knowledge management systems.

Looking Ahead

As the demand for efficient, ethical, and widely accessible AI grows, compact language models are poised to play a central role in shaping the future of artificial intelligence. Their ability to deliver "big results" without the need for "big hardware" ensures their relevance in diverse applications, from personal devices to large-scale enterprise systems.

HISTORICAL CONTEXT: FROM LARGE TO SMALL MODELS

The journey of artificial intelligence, particularly in natural language processing (NLP), has seen a dramatic evolution from rule-based systems to large neural networks and, more recently, to compact and efficient AI models. This progression reflects the growing demand for AI systems that balance performance, accessibility, and sustainability.

The Era of Large Models

1. **Early Beginnings**:
   - Early NLP systems were rule-based, relying on pre-defined grammars and logical constructs. These systems, while innovative, lacked flexibility and adaptability.
2. **The Rise of Statistical Models**:
   - With advancements in computational power, statistical approaches such as Hidden Markov Models (HMMs) and n-grams emerged. These models introduced probabilistic methods for language understanding but were limited by the availability of large datasets.

3. **The Deep Learning Revolution**:
   - The advent of deep learning marked a transformative era. Neural networks, particularly those based on Recurrent Neural Networks (RNNs) and Long Short-Term Memory (LSTM) models, became the backbone of modern NLP.
   - Large pre-trained models like GPT-2, GPT-3, BERT, and T5 set benchmarks for performance, showcasing unprecedented language understanding and generation capabilities.
   - However, these models required extensive computational resources, making them inaccessible for smaller organizations and raising concerns about scalability and environmental impact.

The Shift Toward Smaller Models

1. **Recognition of Challenges with Large Models**:
   - **Resource Intensiveness**: Large models demanded significant computational power for training and deployment, limiting their practical utility.
   - **Latency Issues**: Real-time applications, such as conversational AI and edge computing, struggled with the high latency of large models.
   - **Environmental Costs**: The energy consumption and carbon footprint of training large models became a growing concern.
2. **Emerging Needs for Compact Solutions**:
   - The push for deploying AI in low-resource

environments (e.g., smartphones, IoT devices) highlighted the need for smaller models that could operate effectively with limited computational capacity.

- Applications in underserved regions and industries required lightweight AI systems that maintained high accuracy despite size constraints.

3. **Development of Compact AI Techniques**:
    - Researchers began exploring techniques to reduce the size of large models without compromising performance:
        - **Pruning**: Removing unnecessary parameters to simplify models.
        - **Quantization**: Reducing precision in model computations to lower memory requirements.
        - **Knowledge Distillation**: Training a smaller "student" model to mimic the performance of a larger "teacher" model.
    - Specialized architectures like DistilBERT, MobileBERT, and TinyGPT were developed to address the demand for smaller yet effective models.

From Large to Small: Key Milestones

- **2018**: BERT introduced a transformative approach to language understanding, setting a high-performance standard.
- **2019**: DistilBERT demonstrated that smaller models could retain much of the original BERT's accuracy while being significantly more efficient.
- **2020 and Beyond**: Models like TinyBERT, MobileBERT, and ALBERT pushed the boundaries

of compact AI, proving their capability in both academic and industrial applications.

Modern Implications

Today, the shift from large to small models is not merely a technological adjustment but a response to practical, ethical, and environmental needs. Compact AI models have democratized access to AI, enabling diverse applications ranging from personalized healthcare to real-time language translation on edge devices.

This historical trajectory highlights how innovation in AI is not just about achieving greater power but also about making that power more efficient, accessible, and sustainable.

UNDERSTANDING SMALL LANGUAGE MODELS: DEFINITION AND CHARACTERISTICS

Definition of Small Language Models

Small language models (SLMs) are a subset of artificial intelligence models designed to process and understand natural language with significantly reduced computational and memory requirements compared to large-scale models like GPT-3 or BERT. Despite their compact size, SLMs aim to deliver high performance across various language-related tasks, making them ideal for resource-constrained environments and real-time applications.

Characteristics of Small Language Models

1. **Compact Size**
    - SLMs have fewer parameters, often ranging from millions to a few hundred million, compared to billions in larger models.
    - This reduction in size allows them to require less storage space and computational power.

2. **Optimized Efficiency**
    - Designed to operate efficiently on low-resource devices, such as smartphones, edge devices, or IoT systems.
    - They balance performance with speed, ensuring quick response times in real-time applications.
3. **Cost-Effectiveness**
    - Lower computational requirements translate to reduced energy consumption and operating costs.
    - Training and deployment are more affordable, making them accessible for startups, researchers, and organizations with limited budgets.
4. **Specialized Functionality**
    - Many small language models are task-specific or domain-focused, tailored to excel in particular use cases such as sentiment analysis, summarization, or translation.
    - By focusing on specific tasks, they can achieve high accuracy despite their smaller size.
5. **Energy Efficiency**
    - Smaller models consume significantly less energy during both training and inference, contributing to greener AI solutions.
    - Their reduced carbon footprint aligns with global sustainability goals.
6. **Scalability and Accessibility**
    - Compact size enables deployment on a wide range of devices, extending AI capabilities to underserved regions and low-resource

settings.

- They play a crucial role in democratizing AI, making advanced language processing tools available to a broader audience.

7. **Simplified Maintenance**
    - Easier to update, fine-tune, and manage compared to larger models.
    - Quicker adaptation to new data or specific user requirements.

Comparing Small and Large Language Models

Aspect	Small Models	Large Models
Parameter Count	Millions to a few hundred million	Billions
Computational Needs	Low	High
Training Cost	Affordable	Expensive
Deployment	Suitable for edge devices	Requires high-end hardware
Accuracy	Task-specific, may vary	Generally higher but resource-intensive
Energy Use	Low	High

Popular Examples of Small Language Models

1. **DistilBERT**: A smaller version of BERT that retains 97% of its performance while being 60% faster.
2. **TinyBERT**: Focused on compressing BERT for even greater efficiency.
3. **MobileBERT**: Tailored for mobile and edge device deployment, offering high accuracy at low resource consumption.
4. **ELECTRA-Small**: Designed for efficient training and inference with high accuracy for smaller datasets.

Real-World Relevance

Small language models are becoming essential as industries and developers prioritize efficiency, cost-effectiveness, and sustainability. By bridging the gap between high-performance language processing and practical usability, these models are revolutionizing AI applications across domains such as healthcare, education, business, and beyond.

KEY DIFFERENCES BETWEEN LARGE AND SMALL LANGUAGE MODELS

Large and small language models are both pivotal in natural language processing (NLP) but serve different purposes based on their size, computational requirements, and applications. Understanding their distinctions is crucial for selecting the right model for specific use cases.

---

1. Size of Parameters

- **Large Models**:
  - Typically consist of billions of parameters.
  - Examples: GPT-3 (175 billion parameters), BERT-Large (340 million parameters).
  - Require substantial memory and storage space.
- **Small Models**:
  - Range from millions to a few hundred million parameters.
  - Examples: DistilBERT (66 million parameters), MobileBERT (25 million parameters).
  - Optimized for compactness without compromising significantly on accuracy.

---

2. Computational Resource Requirements

- **Large Models**:
  - Require high-end GPUs, TPUs, or server clusters for training and inference.
  - High computational power results in increased latency for real-time applications.
- **Small Models**:
  - Can run on consumer-grade hardware or edge devices like smartphones and IoT systems.
  - Low latency makes them suitable for real-time and lightweight applications.

---

3. Training and Deployment Costs

- **Large Models**:
  - Training costs are immense, often requiring millions of dollars in resources.
  - Deployment incurs high operational expenses due to power and hardware needs.
- **Small Models**:
  - Training is cost-effective and feasible for smaller organizations or research groups.
  - Deployment is economical, making AI accessible in low-resource settings.

---

4. Performance vs. Task Specificity

- **Large Models**:
  - General-purpose models capable of excelling in a wide range of tasks.
  - Superior performance in handling complex language tasks or nuanced contexts.
- **Small Models**:
  - Typically optimized for specific tasks (e.g., sentiment analysis, translation).
  - May sacrifice some generalization ability for

efficiency in focused applications.

---

5. Energy Consumption and Environmental Impact

- **Large Models**:
  - High energy demands contribute to a larger carbon footprint during training and operation.
  - Environmental concerns are a significant drawback.
- **Small Models**:
  - Consume less energy, making them more sustainable and eco-friendly.
  - Suitable for organizations prioritizing green AI practices.

---

6. Scalability and Accessibility

- **Large Models**:
  - Scalability is often limited by hardware and infrastructure requirements.
  - Accessibility is restricted to well-funded entities such as big tech companies.
- **Small Models**:
  - Easily scalable for various applications across diverse hardware environments.
  - Democratize AI by enabling use in resource-constrained or developing regions.

---

7. Use Cases

- **Large Models**:
  - Research-intensive projects, complex data analysis, and exploratory tasks.
  - Applications demanding deep contextual understanding or high accuracy, such as legal or medical NLP.
- **Small Models**:

- Real-time applications like chatbots, virtual assistants, and embedded AI systems.
- Focused tasks where computational efficiency is paramount.

---

8. Development and Maintenance

- **Large Models**:
  - Difficult to fine-tune or update due to their size and complexity.
  - Maintenance demands extensive expertise and resources.
- **Small Models**:
  - Easier to fine-tune and customize for specific needs.
  - Require minimal resources and expertise for updates.

Summary Table

Aspect	Large Models	Small Models
Parameter Count	Billions	Millions to hundreds of millions
Computational Needs	High	Low
Cost	Expensive	Affordable
Performance	Broad and robust	Task-specific and efficient
Energy Use	High	Low
Deployment	Requires advanced infrastructure	Deployable on edge and consumer devices
Adaptability	Complex fine-tuning	Easily fine-tuned

Small language models are becoming the preferred choice in many scenarios due to their efficiency, cost-effectiveness, and environmental advantages. While large models excel in complex, high-performance tasks, small models are democratizing AI, enabling broader adoption and accessibility.

Technical Foundations: Core Architecture of Small Language Models

Small language models (SLMs) leverage advanced machine learning techniques to achieve efficient language understanding and generation while maintaining a compact size. Their architecture builds on the foundational principles of larger models but incorporates optimizations to balance performance with computational efficiency.

---

1. Core Components of Small Language Models

SLMs share many architectural features with their larger counterparts, such as transformers, attention mechanisms, and embeddings, but with modifications to reduce complexity and size.

- **Embedding Layer**
    - Maps words, subwords, or tokens into dense vector representations.
    - In SLMs, the embedding layer is often compressed or trained with fewer parameters to save memory.
- **Transformer Architecture**
    - Most SLMs are based on the transformer model, which includes:
        - **Self-Attention Mechanism**: Captures relationships between tokens in a sequence.
        - **Feedforward Neural Networks**: Processes contextualized token embeddings.
    - In SLMs, the number of attention heads and

transformer layers is typically reduced.

- **Positional Encoding**
    - Adds information about the order of tokens in a sequence.
    - Simplified positional encodings may be used to reduce computational overhead.

---

2. Techniques for Model Size Reduction

Several strategies are applied to optimize the architecture of SLMs:

- **Knowledge Distillation**
    - A "teacher" model (larger, pre-trained model) transfers its knowledge to a "student" model (smaller).
    - The student model learns to mimic the outputs of the teacher, achieving similar performance with fewer parameters.
- **Parameter Sharing**
    - Layers or weights are shared across the model to reduce the total number of parameters.
    - For example, ALBERT (A Lite BERT) uses shared parameters across transformer layers to achieve compactness.
- **Pruning**
    - Removes redundant or less impactful weights and neurons after initial training.
    - Helps in reducing computational complexity without a significant loss in accuracy.
- **Quantization**
    - Reduces the precision of weights and activations (e.g., from 32-bit floating-point to 8-bit integers).
    - Improves inference speed and reduces memory usage.

---

3. Architectural Variants in Small Models

Different small models use architectural tweaks tailored to specific use cases:

- **DistilBERT**
  - Retains 60% of the layers of BERT while achieving 97% of its performance.
  - Optimized using knowledge distillation and reduced transformer layers.
- **TinyBERT**
  - Employs aggressive pruning and a specialized teacher-student learning framework.
  - Balances size reduction with minimal performance degradation.
- **MobileBERT**
  - Optimized for mobile and edge devices with a narrower and deeper architecture.
  - Uses bottleneck structures to maintain high performance in a compact form.

---

4. Computational Efficiency Techniques

SLMs incorporate design choices to minimize resource usage:

- **Sparse Attention**
  - Focuses computation on relevant parts of the input sequence rather than the entire sequence.
  - Reduces the computational complexity of the self-attention mechanism.
- **Lightweight Feedforward Networks**
  - Replaces fully connected layers with lighter alternatives, such as grouped convolutions or low-rank approximations.
- **Low-Resource Training Techniques**
  - Leveraging transfer learning to pre-train on large datasets and fine-tune on smaller

datasets.

---

5. Training and Fine-Tuning

Training small language models involves techniques that maximize learning efficiency:

- **Pre-training on Large Corpora**
    - Models are first pre-trained on massive datasets using unsupervised tasks like masked language modeling.
- **Task-Specific Fine-Tuning**
    - After pre-training, the model is fine-tuned on domain-specific data to optimize it for tasks like sentiment analysis or summarization.

---

6. Advantages of Small Model Architectures

- **Low Latency**: Streamlined architectures allow real-time processing.
- **Energy Efficiency**: Reduced parameter counts lower computational and energy demands.
- **Versatility**: Easily adaptable to a wide range of applications without requiring extensive resources.

Small language models are a testament to the innovation in AI design, where smart architectural choices ensure that compact models deliver impactful results. Their technical foundation enables efficient and accessible NLP solutions, driving their growing adoption across industries.

Technical Foundations: Techniques for Model Compression (Pruning, Quantization, Distillation)

Model compression techniques are essential for optimizing language models, especially small language models (SLMs). These techniques reduce the size and computational demands of models while maintaining performance, enabling their deployment on resource-constrained devices like smartphones and IoT systems.

---

1. Pruning

Definition: Pruning involves identifying and removing redundant or less significant weights, neurons, or connections from a model. The goal is to simplify the model without significantly affecting its performance.

Types of Pruning:

- **Weight Pruning**:
  - Eliminates individual weights in the model that have minimal impact on its output.
  - Example: Removing weights close to zero.
- **Neuron Pruning**:
  - Removes entire neurons or channels in the network.
  - Particularly effective in convolutional and fully connected layers.
- **Structured Pruning**:
  - Targets specific groups, like layers or blocks, for removal.
  - Easier to implement in hardware than unstructured pruning.

Benefits:

- Reduces model size and inference time.
- Maintains performance when applied carefully.

Challenges:

- Over-pruning can degrade model accuracy.
- Requires careful tuning and validation to identify

what to prune.

---

2. Quantization

Definition: Quantization reduces the precision of numerical representations in the model, such as weights and activations, from high precision (e.g., 32-bit floating-point) to lower precision (e.g., 8-bit integers).

Types of Quantization:

- **Post-Training Quantization (PTQ)**:
  - Applied after the model is trained.
  - Simple and quick, but may result in a minor loss of accuracy.
- **Quantization-Aware Training (QAT)**:
  - Incorporates quantization effects during training.
  - Produces higher-quality compressed models at the cost of additional training time.

Benefits:

- Significant reduction in memory usage.
- Faster inference due to reduced computational complexity.

Challenges:

- Quantization can lead to numerical instability and reduced accuracy, particularly for sensitive tasks.

---

3. Knowledge Distillation

Definition: Knowledge distillation involves training a smaller "student" model to replicate the behavior of a larger "teacher" model. The student model learns from the teacher's predictions rather than the original data.

Steps in Knowledge Distillation:

1. Train the large teacher model on the full dataset.

2. Use the teacher model to generate "soft labels" (probabilistic outputs) for the training data.
3. Train the student model to match the teacher's outputs.

Types of Distillation:

- **Logit Matching**:
  - The student model mimics the teacher's output probabilities.
- **Feature Distillation**:
  - The student model also learns intermediate feature representations from the teacher.

Benefits:

- Produces highly efficient student models with near-teacher-level performance.
- Retains the flexibility to specialize student models for specific tasks.

Challenges:

- The quality of the student model depends on the effectiveness of the teacher model.
- Requires significant computational resources to train the teacher model initially.

---

4. Combined Approaches

Using these techniques in combination can amplify their benefits:

- **Pruning + Quantization**: Prune the model first to reduce its size and then apply quantization to further optimize for memory and speed.
- **Distillation + Quantization**: Use knowledge distillation to train a smaller student model and then quantize it for deployment.

Summary Table

Technique	Primary Goal	Advantages	Challenges
Pruning	Remove redundant model components	Smaller model size, faster inference	Risk of accuracy degradation, requires fine-tuning
Quantization	Reduce numerical precision	Lower memory usage, faster computations	Potential loss of accuracy, numerical instability
Distillation	Transfer knowledge to smaller model	Near-teacher performance, task flexibility	High teacher training cost, requires additional data

Impact on Small Language Models

Small language models benefit immensely from these compression techniques:

- **Practical Deployment**: Compression enables deployment on edge devices and in real-time systems.
- **Energy Efficiency**: Lower computational requirements reduce energy consumption.
- **Accessibility**: Smaller, efficient models democratize AI applications for diverse users and regions.

By applying these techniques, small language models can achieve "big results" while operating under stringent resource constraints.

TECHNICAL FOUNDATIONS: TECHNIQUES FOR MODEL COMPRESSION (PRUNING, QUANTIZATION, DISTILLATION)

Model compression techniques play a crucial role in making machine learning models smaller, faster, and more efficient without compromising their accuracy significantly. These techniques are particularly vital for Small Language Models (SLMs), enabling their deployment in resource-constrained environments like mobile devices, IoT, and edge computing.

---

1. Pruning

Definition: Pruning involves identifying and removing parts of a neural network, such as weights, neurons, or even layers, that contribute minimally to the model's output.

Types of Pruning:

1. **Weight Pruning**
    - Removes individual weights that have little impact on predictions.
    - Focuses on sparsity at the level of individual connections.
2. **Neuron Pruning**
    - Eliminates entire neurons or channels that are deemed redundant.
    - Simplifies the network while maintaining functionality.
3. **Structured Pruning**
    - Removes predefined components like filters, heads, or blocks, making it hardware-friendly.

How It Works:

- A fully trained model is analyzed to determine which components contribute least to overall accuracy.
- These components are removed, and the model is fine-tuned to recover lost performance.

Advantages:

- Reduces model size and computational complexity.
- Faster inference speeds with minimal impact on accuracy (if applied judiciously).

Challenges:

- Over-pruning can degrade performance.
- Requires iterative evaluation and tuning.

---

2. Quantization

Definition: Quantization reduces the precision of numerical computations in a model, such as weights, biases, and activations, to save memory and accelerate computations.

Types of Quantization:

1. **Post-Training Quantization (PTQ)**
    - Applied after the model is fully trained.
    - Converts 32-bit floating-point weights into lower precision (e.g., 8-bit integers).
2. **Quantization-Aware Training (QAT)**
    - Simulates quantized operations during training.
    - Leads to better accuracy compared to PTQ but requires additional computational resources.

How It Works:

- Precision is reduced while maintaining dynamic ranges to represent values effectively.
- Popular techniques include fixed-point arithmetic and mixed-precision training.

Advantages:

- Significant reduction in model size and memory footprint.
- Faster inference due to simpler arithmetic operations.

Challenges:

- Can lead to numerical instability and accuracy loss, particularly for sensitive tasks.
- Fine-tuning may be needed after quantization.

---

3. Knowledge Distillation

Definition: Knowledge distillation involves training a smaller "student" model to learn from a larger, pre-trained "teacher" model. The student model mimics the teacher's predictions and behavior.

How It Works:

1. The teacher model generates "soft labels" (probability distributions) for the training data.
2. The student model is trained to replicate the teacher's outputs, rather than directly learning from the dataset.

Variants:

1. **Logit Distillation**
    - Focuses on matching the teacher's probability distribution at the output layer.
2. **Feature-Based Distillation**
    - The student learns intermediate representations from the teacher.

Advantages:

- Produces smaller models with near-teacher-level performance.
- Reduces the dependency on large datasets during training.

Challenges:

- The quality of the student model depends on the teacher's accuracy.
- Training requires significant computational resources initially for the teacher model.

---

4. Combined Approaches

These compression techniques are often combined for better results:

- **Pruning + Quantization**: Remove redundant components through pruning, then reduce numerical precision via quantization.

- **Distillation + Quantization**: Train a smaller student model using distillation, followed by quantization for deployment.
- **Pruning + Distillation**: Simplify the teacher model using pruning, then transfer knowledge to the student model.

Benefits of Model Compression

- **Efficiency**: Smaller models require less memory and computational power, making them ideal for edge devices.
- **Cost-Effectiveness**: Reduced energy and hardware costs for training and deployment.
- **Accessibility**: Enables AI deployment in low-resource environments, democratizing access to AI technologies.

Impact on Small Language Models

Model compression techniques empower Small Language Models to deliver high performance despite resource constraints. This makes them:

- **Deployable on Edge Devices**: Fit for real-time applications on smartphones, wearables, and IoT systems.
- **Energy Efficient**: Reduced computational requirements lower energy consumption.
- **Scalable**: Easier to train, fine-tune, and deploy for diverse applications, from chatbots to real-time translation tools.

By leveraging pruning, quantization, and knowledge distillation, SLMs achieve "big results" while staying compact and efficient.

TECHNICAL FOUNDATIONS: TRAINING AND OPTIMIZATION CHALLENGES

Training and optimizing small language models (SLMs) present unique challenges compared to their larger counterparts. The goal is to achieve high accuracy, efficiency, and generalization while working within the constraints of limited parameters and computational resources. This section explores these challenges and approaches to address them.

---

1. Limited Model Capacity

Small language models have fewer parameters, which limits their ability to capture complex relationships in data.

Challenges:

- Struggles to generalize in scenarios involving large datasets or diverse tasks.
- Risk of underfitting due to insufficient representation power.

Solutions:

- **Task-Specific Fine-Tuning**: Train the model on data

tailored to specific applications.

- **Knowledge Distillation**: Use a larger teacher model to guide the training of the smaller model.
- **Architectural Innovations**: Incorporate efficient design choices such as attention mechanisms and modular networks.

---

2. Computational Efficiency vs. Accuracy Trade-offs

Smaller models are designed for efficiency but often at the cost of accuracy.

Challenges:

- Maintaining high performance while adhering to hardware and latency constraints.
- Balancing inference speed and accuracy, especially for real-time applications.

Solutions:

- **Dynamic Inference**: Use adaptive computation techniques, such as skipping layers or conditionally activating parts of the model.
- **Quantization-Aware Training**: Maintain precision during training to reduce accuracy loss from quantization.

---

3. Data Availability and Quality

Training effective small models requires high-quality data, but obtaining sufficient data for diverse tasks can be challenging.

Challenges:

- Small models may struggle with limited or noisy datasets.
- Performance degrades when transferring to domains with little training data.

Solutions:

- **Data Augmentation**: Expand datasets with synthetic examples or transformations.
- **Transfer Learning**: Pre-train models on large datasets before fine-tuning them for specific tasks.
- **Few-Shot and Zero-Shot Learning**: Optimize the model to perform well with minimal labeled data.

---

4. Optimization Difficulties

Training small models involves finding a balance between underfitting and overfitting, which can be difficult given their limited complexity.

Challenges:

- Narrow optimization landscapes make convergence harder.
- Overfitting to small datasets due to fewer parameters being overly tuned.

Solutions:

- **Regularization Techniques**: Use dropout, weight decay, and early stopping to prevent overfitting.
- **Learning Rate Schedules**: Apply dynamic learning rates to ensure stable convergence.
- **Gradient Clipping**: Prevent exploding gradients during optimization.

---

5. Scalability and Hardware Constraints

Small models are often deployed on resource-limited devices, such as edge systems, smartphones, and IoT devices.

Challenges:

- Ensuring compatibility with low-power hardware.
- Managing memory and computational constraints

during training and inference.

Solutions:

- **Efficient Architectures**: Utilize lightweight designs like MobileNet and TinyBERT.
- **Model Compression**: Apply pruning, quantization, or weight sharing to reduce memory usage.
- **Distributed Training**: Use parallel and federated learning for scalable model training.

---

6. Robustness and Generalization

Small models are prone to brittleness when encountering adversarial inputs or shifting data distributions.

Challenges:

- Vulnerability to adversarial attacks and biases.
- Poor generalization across different domains or languages.

Solutions:

- **Adversarial Training**: Introduce adversarial examples during training to improve robustness.
- **Domain Adaptation**: Use transfer learning to fine-tune models for new domains.
- **Cross-Lingual Pre-training**: Train on multilingual datasets to improve generalization across languages.

---

7. Evaluation and Fine-Tuning Metrics

Measuring the effectiveness of training and fine-tuning for small models poses unique difficulties.

Challenges:

- Standard evaluation metrics may not reflect real-world performance.

- Task-specific requirements may vary significantly.

Solutions:

- **Task-Specific Metrics**: Use precision, recall, F1 score, and BLEU score for task relevance.
- **Holistic Benchmarks**: Employ benchmarks like GLUE and SuperGLUE to evaluate performance comprehensively.
- **Real-World Testing**: Deploy small models in production environments to assess their practical usability.

Conclusion

Training and optimizing small language models require innovative techniques to address their inherent limitations. By tackling challenges related to capacity, efficiency, data, optimization, and deployment, researchers and practitioners can ensure these compact AI systems achieve "big results" in real-world applications.

APPLICATIONS IN NATURAL LANGUAGE PROCESSING: TEXT CLASSIFICATION AND SENTIMENT ANALYSIS

Text classification and sentiment analysis are among the most prominent applications of natural language processing (NLP). Small language models (SLMs) excel in these tasks, offering efficient, scalable solutions that are well-suited for deployment in real-world scenarios, particularly on resource-constrained devices.

---

1. Text Classification

Definition:
Text classification involves organizing text into predefined categories based on its content. Applications range from spam filtering to news categorization and beyond.

How Small Language Models Are Used:

- **Feature Extraction**: SLMs encode input text into vectors representing semantic meaning.
- **Prediction Layer**: A lightweight classifier (e.g.,

softmax or linear layer) maps these representations to categories.

Advantages of SLMs:

- Low latency and faster inference speeds.
- Reduced computational and memory requirements, enabling deployment on edge devices.
- Easier fine-tuning for domain-specific tasks due to their smaller size.

Example Use Cases:

1. **Spam Detection**: Classify emails or messages as spam or not.
2. **News Categorization**: Organize articles into categories like sports, technology, or health.
3. **Topic Modeling**: Assign topics to large volumes of text data for research or analysis.

---

2. Sentiment Analysis

Definition:
Sentiment analysis involves detecting the emotional tone of a piece of text, categorizing it as positive, negative, or neutral.

How Small Language Models Are Used:

- **Token Embeddings**: SLMs tokenize and process input text, capturing emotional and contextual signals.
- **Sentiment Scoring**: The model outputs sentiment scores or probabilities for each class.

Advantages of SLMs:

- **Faster Training and Inference**: Ideal for large-scale customer reviews or social media data.
- **Scalability**: Can be deployed across multiple platforms, such as mobile apps or web APIs.
- **Real-Time Analysis**: Enables businesses to monitor

customer feedback instantly.

Example Use Cases:

1. **Product Reviews**: Analyze customer feedback to understand satisfaction and identify areas for improvement.
2. **Social Media Monitoring**: Track public sentiment during events, elections, or brand campaigns.
3. **Customer Support**: Detect negative sentiment in support tickets for prioritization.

Techniques Leveraged by Small Language Models

1. Pre-training and Fine-tuning:

SLMs, pre-trained on general text corpora, can be fine-tuned on task-specific datasets for text classification or sentiment analysis.

2. Task-Specific Layers:

Adding lightweight classification heads allows SLMs to adapt to specific text processing tasks efficiently.

3. Domain Adaptation:

SLMs can be fine-tuned with domain-specific vocabulary and data, enhancing their accuracy in niche applications like medical or legal text classification.

Challenges and Solutions

Challenges:

1. **Limited Context Understanding**: SLMs may struggle with long or complex inputs.
2. **Domain Shift**: Performance may degrade on data outside the training domain.
3. **Ambiguity in Sentiment**: Sarcasm, irony, or mixed emotions can be difficult to interpret.

Solutions:

- Use **text chunking** or hierarchical models to handle long inputs.
- Apply **transfer learning** for domain adaptation.
- Enhance training datasets with examples of ambiguous or complex sentiment.

Conclusion

Small language models are powerful tools for text classification and sentiment analysis. By leveraging their efficiency, businesses and developers can deploy scalable solutions across a variety of domains. Despite their compact size, SLMs achieve remarkable accuracy, enabling real-time and resource-efficient NLP applications that deliver "big results."

APPLICATIONS IN NATURAL LANGUAGE PROCESSING: MACHINE TRANSLATION WITH COMPACT MODELS

Machine translation (MT) aims to automatically convert text from one language to another while preserving meaning, tone, and context. Traditionally dominated by large language models (LLMs), compact models are increasingly being employed in this field due to their efficiency and suitability for low-resource environments.

---

1. Overview of Machine Translation with Compact Models

Compact models use smaller architectures with fewer parameters, focusing on maintaining translation accuracy while optimizing resource usage. These models leverage advancements like knowledge distillation, pruning, and quantization to deliver high-quality translations with reduced computational requirements.

---

2. Techniques Used by Compact Models in Machine

Translation

1. Knowledge Distillation

- A large teacher model is used to train a smaller student model, transferring knowledge while reducing the size and complexity.
- Improves the ability of compact models to capture linguistic nuances and syntax.

2. Subword Tokenization

- Methods like Byte Pair Encoding (BPE) and SentencePiece break text into subword units.
- Reduces vocabulary size while enabling the model to handle rare and unseen words effectively.

3. Shared Encoder-Decoder Frameworks

- Lightweight transformer-based architectures share weights across encoder and decoder layers to minimize memory usage.
- Increases efficiency without a significant loss in performance.

---

3. Advantages of Using Compact Models in Machine Translation

1. Resource Efficiency

- Suitable for deployment on edge devices like mobile phones and IoT systems.
- Requires less computational power and memory, reducing infrastructure costs.

2. Faster Inference Times

- Compact models process input text more quickly, enabling real-time translation applications.

3. Accessibility for Low-Resource Languages

- Efficient training allows compact models to perform well even in languages with limited parallel corpora.

4. Scalability

- Their smaller size makes it feasible to deploy multiple models for various language pairs on a single device or platform.

---

4. Example Applications

1. Real-Time Translation Apps

- Compact models enable real-time text and voice translation in apps like Google Translate and Microsoft Translator on mobile devices.

2. Translation for Low-Resource Languages

- Compact models are instrumental in providing MT services for languages with limited digital resources, promoting inclusivity.

3. On-Device Translation

- Models like OpenNMT and MarianMT have lightweight versions that operate offline, ensuring privacy and accessibility.

4. Industry-Specific Translation

- Tailored compact models can translate specialized text, such as legal documents or medical records, with domain-specific fine-tuning.

---

5. Challenges and Solutions

1. Limited Context Understanding

- Compact models may struggle to maintain coherence in long sentences or paragraphs.
  Solution: Use segment-level translation combined with contextual embeddings.

2. Trade-offs in Accuracy

- Reducing model size can result in loss of translation quality.
  Solution: Apply techniques like knowledge distillation and fine-tuning on task-specific data.

3. Handling Ambiguity and Idioms

- Compact models often fail to interpret idiomatic expressions correctly.
  Solution: Enrich training datasets with idiomatic and colloquial examples.

---

6. Popular Compact Models for Machine Translation

1. MarianMT

- An open-source MT model optimized for low-resource settings.
- Offers pre-trained models for various language pairs.

2. TinyBERT

- Uses a distilled transformer architecture for lightweight translation tasks.

3. Quantized Transformer Models

- Utilizes quantization techniques to reduce memory usage without compromising quality.

---

7. Future Directions

1. Multilingual Compact Models

- Single models capable of translating between multiple language pairs efficiently.

2. Federated Learning

- Collaborative model training across devices to improve translation for local dialects while preserving privacy.

3. Hybrid Approaches

- Combining compact models with rule-based or statistical techniques to improve accuracy and domain-specific performance.

Conclusion

Compact models are revolutionizing machine translation by balancing efficiency and performance. While they may not yet match the quality of larger models in all scenarios, their advantages in resource efficiency, scalability, and accessibility make them a vital tool in democratizing translation services.

APPLICATIONS IN NATURAL LANGUAGE PROCESSING: SUMMARIZATION AND KEYWORD EXTRACTION

Summarization and keyword extraction are critical tasks in natural language processing (NLP), providing concise, actionable insights from vast amounts of text data. Small language models (SLMs) are particularly suited for these tasks due to their efficiency and ability to deliver meaningful results while minimizing resource usage.

---

1. Summarization

Definition:
Summarization involves generating a concise version of a text while retaining the most important information.

Types of Summarization:

1. **Extractive Summarization**:
    - Selects key sentences or phrases directly from the source text.
    - Example: Highlighting key points in a news

article.

2. **Abstractive Summarization**:
   - Generates new sentences that convey the essence of the source text, often rephrasing or condensing ideas.
   - Example: Creating a brief summary for a research paper.

How Small Language Models Are Used:

- **Input Processing**: SLMs tokenize the text into smaller units (words or subwords).
- **Content Identification**: Models identify the most relevant parts of the text using learned patterns and contextual embeddings.
- **Output Generation**: Depending on the task, they either extract key sentences (extractive) or generate concise paraphrased content (abstractive).

Advantages of SLMs for Summarization:

- **Efficiency**: Processes text quickly, even on resource-constrained devices.
- **Domain Adaptability**: Easily fine-tuned for specific use cases like legal, medical, or technical domains.
- **Cost-Effectiveness**: Requires fewer computational resources for training and inference compared to larger models.

Example Use Cases:

1. **News Summarization**: Generating short summaries for news feeds.
2. **Meeting Notes**: Condensing meeting transcripts into actionable points.
3. **Research Summaries**: Simplifying academic papers for broader audiences.

2. Keyword Extraction

Definition:
Keyword extraction identifies the most significant words or phrases in a text that represent its primary themes or topics.

How Small Language Models Are Used:

- **Contextual Understanding**: Models analyze the text to determine the importance of each token in its context.
- **Scoring and Selection**: Assign scores to tokens based on frequency, importance, and contextual relevance, then extract top-ranking keywords.

Advantages of SLMs for Keyword Extraction:

- **Accuracy**: Provides context-aware keyword selection, unlike simple statistical methods.
- **Scalability**: Handles large volumes of text efficiently.
- **Multilingual Capability**: Supports keyword extraction in multiple languages when appropriately fine-tuned.

Example Use Cases:

1. **Search Engine Optimization (SEO)**: Extracting keywords from web content for optimization.
2. **Content Indexing**: Generating tags for articles, blogs, or media content.
3. **Market Research**: Analyzing customer feedback to identify recurring themes.

Techniques Leveraged by Small Language Models

1. Fine-Tuning:

SLMs can be fine-tuned on domain-specific datasets to improve summarization or keyword extraction performance.

2. Attention Mechanisms:

Lightweight attention mechanisms help SLMs focus on the most relevant parts of the input text.

3. Integration with Statistical Methods:

Combining SLMs with traditional methods like Term Frequency-Inverse Document Frequency (TF-IDF) can enhance performance, particularly for keyword extraction.

Challenges and Solutions

Challenges:

1. **Loss of Context in Long Texts**: Summarization and keyword extraction might miss important nuances.
   Solution: Use hierarchical or multi-pass approaches to divide and process long texts.
2. **Ambiguity in Keywords**: Extracted keywords might not always align with the user's intent.
   Solution: Include task-specific or user-defined constraints during training.
3. **Abstractive Summarization Complexity**: Small models may generate incomplete or inaccurate summaries.
   Solution: Enhance training data diversity and apply reinforcement learning for better quality.

Future Trends

1. **Hybrid Approaches**: Combining SLMs with rule-based methods for improved accuracy in domain-specific tasks.
2. **On-Device Applications**: Using compact models for summarization and keyword extraction directly on mobile or IoT devices.
3. **Multimodal Summarization**: Extending capabilities

to process text, images, and audio inputs for more comprehensive summaries.

Conclusion

Summarization and keyword extraction demonstrate the potential of small language models to distill critical information efficiently. By optimizing these tasks, SLMs empower industries ranging from journalism to business intelligence, proving that compact AI solutions can achieve big results.

ENTERPRISE AND COMMERCIAL USE CASES: CUSTOMER SERVICE AUTOMATION

Customer service automation is a critical area where small language models (SLMs) shine, delivering personalized, efficient, and resource-friendly solutions. By leveraging SLMs, businesses can streamline operations, reduce costs, and enhance customer satisfaction without the heavy computational demands of larger models.

---

1. Overview of Customer Service Automation

Customer service automation involves using AI-driven tools to handle routine inquiries, assist with troubleshooting, and provide 24/7 support. Small language models enable these functionalities through chatbots, virtual assistants, and ticketing systems optimized for fast and accurate responses.

---

2. Applications of SLMs in Customer Service Automation

1. Chatbots and Virtual Assistants

- SLMs power conversational agents that handle customer queries in real time.

- **Example**: Responding to frequently asked questions (FAQs) about account balances, product availability, or delivery status.

2. Automated Ticketing Systems

- Models classify customer issues, prioritize tickets, and route them to the appropriate teams.
- **Example**: Categorizing incoming requests as "technical issue," "billing query," or "general inquiry."

3. Personalized Customer Interactions

- Compact AI tailors responses based on user history and preferences.
- **Example**: Recommending products or services based on past purchases or queries.

4. Multilingual Support

- SLMs trained for translation and multilingual understanding enable businesses to serve global audiences.
- **Example**: Handling queries in multiple languages without needing separate resources for each.

---

3. Advantages of Small Language Models in Customer Service

1. Cost Efficiency

- Lower computational requirements make SLMs affordable to deploy and maintain.

2. Scalability

- Easily scalable to handle varying volumes of customer queries during peak times.

3. On-Device and Edge Deployments

- Operable on lightweight devices, ensuring faster response times and enhanced privacy.

4. Quick Training and Fine-Tuning

- SLMs can be quickly adapted to specific industries, products, or services.

---

4. Challenges and Solutions

1. Limited Context Awareness

- SLMs may struggle with complex or multi-turn conversations.
  Solution: Implement context-tracking mechanisms or integrate with external memory systems.

2. Misinterpretation of Queries

- Smaller models might occasionally misclassify ambiguous customer inputs.
  Solution: Use hybrid models combining rule-based systems with SLMs for improved accuracy.

3. Handling Sensitive Data

- Data privacy concerns can arise when handling personal customer information.
  Solution: Ensure compliance with data protection standards (e.g., GDPR, HIPAA) and use encrypted data handling.

---

5. Example Use Cases in the Industry

1. E-commerce

- Automated chatbots assist with order tracking, refunds, and product inquiries.
- **Example**: "Your order will arrive on Nov 22. Let me know if you need further assistance!"

2. Banking and Finance

- Virtual assistants guide customers through processes like account setup or loan applications.

- **Example**: "To reset your password, click here or follow these steps."

3. **Healthcare**
    - Automating patient appointment scheduling and answering basic health queries.
    - **Example**: "Your appointment with Dr. Sharma is confirmed for Nov 25 at 10:00 AM."
4. **Telecommunications**
    - Managing technical support queries, like troubleshooting connectivity issues.
    - **Example**: "Have you tried restarting your router? Here's a step-by-step guide."

---

6. Metrics for Success

1. **First Response Time (FRT)**
    - Reduced latency in responding to customer queries.
2. **Customer Satisfaction (CSAT)**
    - Improved ratings due to faster and accurate resolutions.
3. **Cost Per Resolution (CPR)**
    - Lower costs by automating high-volume, low-complexity queries.
4. **Query Deflection Rate**
    - The percentage of inquiries resolved without human intervention.

---

7. Future Trends in Customer Service Automation with SLMs

1. **Emotionally Intelligent Bots**
    - Incorporating sentiment analysis to tailor responses to customer emotions.

2. Advanced Multimodal Assistance

- Integrating text, voice, and visual inputs for comprehensive support.

3. Proactive Customer Engagement

- Using predictive analytics to address issues before customers reach out.

4. Personalization at Scale

- Combining compact models with customer relationship management (CRM) data for deeper insights.

Conclusion

Customer service automation powered by small language models is transforming how businesses interact with their clients. By making intelligent, personalized assistance accessible even on low-resource platforms, SLMs empower enterprises to deliver exceptional customer experiences while optimizing operational efficiency.

ENTERPRISE AND COMMERCIAL USE CASES: AI-POWERED CRM SYSTEMS

Customer Relationship Management (CRM) systems are essential tools for businesses to manage customer interactions, improve engagement, and drive sales. Integrating small language models (SLMs) into CRM systems enhances their functionality by introducing automation, personalization, and advanced analytics capabilities.

---

1. Overview of AI-Powered CRM Systems

AI-powered CRM systems leverage artificial intelligence to process customer data, predict behavior, and automate routine tasks. Small language models play a pivotal role by enabling real-time natural language understanding, sentiment analysis, and contextual responses, making CRMs more intuitive and effective.

---

2. Features of AI-Powered CRM Systems with SLMs

1. Automated Data Entry and Management

- SLMs process customer emails, chat transcripts, and call logs to populate CRM fields.
- **Example**: Extracting customer details from emails

and updating contact information in the CRM.

2. Sentiment Analysis

- Analyze customer feedback or interactions to gauge sentiment (positive, negative, neutral).
- **Example**: Identifying dissatisfaction in a customer support email to prioritize resolution.

3. Predictive Customer Insights

- Using historical data and behavioral patterns to predict customer needs or actions.
- **Example**: Suggesting upsell opportunities based on past purchases.

4. Intelligent Chatbots and Assistants

- Enhancing customer service by integrating chatbots within CRM platforms for instant query resolution.
- **Example**: "Your last order was placed on Nov 15. Would you like to reorder the same product?"

5. Personalized Communication

- SLMs generate personalized email responses, recommendations, or marketing content.
- **Example**: Crafting emails tailored to customer preferences or purchase history.

6. Multilingual Support

- Enabling global businesses to interact with customers in their native languages.
- **Example**: Auto-translating customer inquiries and responses in the CRM system.

---

3. Benefits of AI-Powered CRM Systems with SLMs

1. Enhanced Productivity

- Automating routine tasks like data entry and follow-ups allows sales and support teams to focus on strategic activities.

2. Better Customer Insights

- Real-time analysis of interactions provides actionable insights, enabling more effective decision-making.

3. Improved Customer Experience

- Faster, more accurate responses and personalized interactions enhance customer satisfaction.

4. Cost Efficiency

- Reduces the need for extensive manual input or large-scale AI infrastructure, as SLMs provide lightweight solutions.

5. Scalability

- Easily adapts to growing customer data and interaction volumes without a proportional increase in resources.

---

4. Challenges and Mitigations

1. Data Privacy Concerns

- Handling sensitive customer data securely is a key challenge.
  Solution: Use on-premise deployments or encrypted cloud solutions compliant with regulations like GDPR.

2. Accuracy in Complex Contexts

- SLMs may occasionally misinterpret nuanced customer queries.
  Solution: Combine SLMs with rule-based systems or train models on domain-specific data.

3. Integration Complexity

- Integrating AI-powered CRMs with existing systems can be challenging.
  Solution: Opt for modular CRM platforms with open APIs to streamline integration.

4. Scalability for Large Data

- While SLMs are efficient, managing very large datasets might require additional optimization.
  Solution: Use hybrid approaches by combining SLMs with traditional data processing pipelines.

---

5. Example Use Cases in Industries

1. Retail and E-commerce

- **Use Case**: Personalized product recommendations and automated follow-up emails.
- **Impact**: Boosts conversion rates and customer loyalty.

2. Banking and Financial Services

- **Use Case**: Managing customer queries related to account details, loan applications, or fraud alerts.
- **Impact**: Reduces customer wait times and improves trust.

3. Healthcare

- **Use Case**: Scheduling appointments and sending personalized health reminders.
- **Impact**: Enhances patient engagement and adherence to care plans.

4. Travel and Hospitality

- **Use Case**: Automating responses to booking inquiries and offering personalized travel recommendations.
- **Impact**: Increases customer satisfaction and retention.

---

6. Metrics for Evaluating Success

1. Customer Satisfaction (CSAT)

- Improved feedback scores due to personalized interactions and quicker resolutions.

2. Sales Conversion Rate

- Increase in conversions driven by personalized recommendations and insights.

3. Operational Efficiency

- Reduction in time spent on manual tasks like data entry or ticket routing.

4. Retention Rate

- Enhanced customer loyalty due to proactive and personalized communication.

---

7. Future Trends in AI-Powered CRM Systems with SLMs

1. Advanced Predictive Analytics

- Leveraging SLMs to anticipate customer churn and recommend retention strategies.

2. Voice-Enabled CRMs

- Enabling sales teams to interact with CRMs through voice commands powered by compact AI.

3. Real-Time Collaboration

- SLMs facilitating seamless collaboration by summarizing customer interactions for team updates.

4. Hyper-Personalization

- Using deeper contextual analysis to customize every aspect of the customer experience.

Conclusion

AI-powered CRM systems enhanced by small language models revolutionize how businesses manage customer relationships. By blending efficiency, personalization, and scalability, these systems empower enterprises to deliver superior customer experiences while optimizing operational workflows. SLMs serve as a cornerstone in making sophisticated CRM tools accessible and impactful across industries.

ENTERPRISE AND COMMERCIAL USE CASES: DOCUMENT PROCESSING AND KNOWLEDGE MANAGEMENT

Document processing and knowledge management are vital for enterprises aiming to organize, retrieve, and utilize information efficiently. Small language models (SLMs) enhance these domains by automating document workflows, enabling intelligent content extraction, and facilitating streamlined knowledge sharing.

---

1. Overview of Document Processing and Knowledge Management

Document processing involves tasks such as classification, summarization, and data extraction from textual content. Knowledge management focuses on creating, sharing, and managing organizational knowledge. SLMs, with their lightweight architecture, make these tasks faster, more accessible, and cost-effective for enterprises.

---

2. Applications of SLMs in Document Processing

1. Document Classification

- Automatically categorizing documents based on content.
- **Example**: Sorting incoming emails as "invoices," "contracts," or "support tickets."

2. Summarization

- Generating concise summaries of lengthy documents.
- **Example**: Summarizing policy documents for quick review by stakeholders.

3. Information Extraction

- Identifying and extracting key data points, such as dates, names, or numerical values.
- **Example**: Extracting invoice numbers and due dates from scanned receipts.

4. OCR and Text Recognition Integration

- Pairing SLMs with Optical Character Recognition (OCR) systems for processing scanned or handwritten documents.
- **Example**: Extracting patient details from handwritten medical forms.

---

3. Applications of SLMs in Knowledge Management

1. Contextual Search

- Enabling employees to find relevant documents or information using natural language queries.
- **Example**: Searching for "latest sales projections for Q4" and retrieving relevant reports.

2. FAQ and Knowledge Base Automation

- Creating and managing FAQ systems by summarizing or paraphrasing knowledge base content.
- **Example**: Generating FAQs for a new product launch based on internal training materials.

3. Document Linking and Cross-Referencing

- Identifying relationships between documents and linking them for easy navigation.
- **Example**: Suggesting related research papers or reports in an academic setting.

4. Real-Time Knowledge Updates

- Updating organizational knowledge bases with the latest extracted information.
- **Example**: Adding new regulatory compliance updates to a company's legal database.

---

4. Advantages of Using SLMs

1. Cost-Effectiveness

- Reduces reliance on large-scale computing resources while delivering effective results.

2. Speed and Scalability

- Quickly processes large volumes of documents, adapting to organizational growth.

3. Accessibility

- Deployable on lightweight devices, making document and knowledge management accessible even in resource-constrained settings.

4. Privacy and Security

- On-device processing ensures sensitive documents remain confidential.

---

5. Challenges and Mitigation Strategies

1. Handling Ambiguous Content

- SLMs may struggle with ambiguous or incomplete information.
  Solution: Use hybrid systems combining SLMs with rule-based approaches for higher accuracy.

2. Maintaining Knowledge Base Accuracy

- Keeping the knowledge base updated and error-free is a challenge.
  Solution: Schedule regular audits and updates of the knowledge repository.

3. Processing Complex Documents

- Legal or technical documents with intricate language can be difficult for SLMs.
  Solution: Fine-tune SLMs with domain-specific datasets for better comprehension.

4. Multilingual Document Handling

- SLMs may not natively support all languages.
  Solution: Train or integrate with multilingual SLMs to process diverse content.

---

6. Industry Use Cases

1. Legal and Compliance

- Automating contract review and compliance checks.
- **Impact**: Reduces manual effort and minimizes risks of overlooking critical clauses.

2. Healthcare

- Extracting patient data from medical records and creating summarized case reports.
- **Impact**: Enhances decision-making and reduces administrative burdens.

3. Finance

- Processing invoices, balance sheets, and financial statements for analysis.
- **Impact**: Streamlines workflows and ensures timely reporting.

4. Education

- Organizing academic research and summarizing scholarly articles.
- **Impact**: Improves accessibility to critical knowledge for researchers and students.

---

7. Metrics for Measuring Success

1. Processing Time

- Reduction in time required to extract and organize document content.

2. Accuracy Rates

- The percentage of correctly classified or extracted information.

3. Knowledge Base Utilization

- The frequency and effectiveness of accessing and using knowledge base content.

4. User Satisfaction

- Employee or customer feedback on the usability and reliability of document and knowledge management systems.

---

8. Future Trends

1. Multimodal Document Processing

- Combining text, images, and videos for comprehensive document analysis.

2. Semantic Knowledge Graphs

- Building interconnected knowledge systems using SLMs for enhanced insights.

3. Adaptive Learning Models

- SLMs that evolve with organizational data and adapt to new formats and structures.

4. Enhanced Collaboration Tools

- Integration of SLMs into team platforms for real-time knowledge sharing.

Conclusion

Small language models are transforming document processing and knowledge management, offering cost-effective, efficient, and scalable solutions for enterprises. By automating routine tasks and enhancing access to organizational knowledge, SLMs empower businesses to focus on strategic objectives while maintaining an edge in information management.

HEALTHCARE INNOVATIONS WITH SMALL AI MODELS: ENHANCING DIAGNOSTICS IN LOW-RESOURCE SETTINGS

Small AI models, with their lightweight and efficient design, are playing an increasingly pivotal role in revolutionizing healthcare diagnostics, especially in low-resource settings. Their ability to operate on limited computational power and provide accurate, real-time analysis makes them invaluable in regions where access to advanced healthcare infrastructure is limited.

---

1. Challenges in Diagnostics in Low-Resource Settings

1. Limited Access to Specialists

- A shortage of trained healthcare professionals, particularly in rural or underserved areas.

2. Inadequate Infrastructure

- Lack of advanced diagnostic tools and reliable internet connectivity.

3. High Costs of Traditional Solutions

- Expensive diagnostic equipment and tools are often unaffordable in these settings.

4. Time Sensitivity

- Delayed diagnostics can lead to poor health outcomes, especially in critical conditions.

---

2. The Role of Small AI Models in Addressing Challenges

1. Offline Functionality

- Small AI models can operate locally on edge devices without requiring internet connectivity.
- **Example**: Portable devices powered by small AI models analyzing X-rays or ultrasound images on-site.

2. Low-Cost Deployment

- These models are computationally efficient and can run on affordable devices like smartphones or Raspberry Pi systems.

3. Quick and Accurate Diagnostics

- Real-time analysis of medical data, enabling faster decision-making.
- **Example**: Rapid detection of conditions like pneumonia or malaria using image analysis.

4. Scalability and Adaptability

- Easy to customize for various medical conditions and integrate into existing workflows.
- **Example**: Adapting models for local languages to assist healthcare workers in remote regions.

---

3. Key Applications of Small AI Models in Low-Resource Diagnostics

1. Image-Based Diagnostics

- Analyzing medical images such as X-rays, CT scans, and ultrasounds.
- **Example**: Identifying signs of tuberculosis or fractures in chest X-rays.

2. Disease Screening and Monitoring

- Early detection of diseases like diabetes, hypertension, or infectious diseases.
- **Example**: Screening for diabetic retinopathy using small models integrated into smartphone apps.

3. Lab Test Interpretation

- Analyzing lab results like blood tests or urine analysis.
- **Example**: Detecting anemia by analyzing hemoglobin levels from basic test data.

4. Remote Patient Monitoring

- Enabling wearable devices to monitor vital signs and detect abnormalities.
- **Example**: Tracking heart rate variability to predict cardiac events.

5. Triage and Decision Support

- Assisting healthcare workers in prioritizing patients based on severity.
- **Example**: Identifying critical cases during outbreaks, such as COVID-19.

---

4. Advantages of Using Small AI Models in Diagnostics

1. Portability

- Compact devices powered by small AI models can be transported easily to remote locations.

2. Energy Efficiency

- Operates with minimal power consumption, ideal for areas with unreliable electricity.

3. Easy Training and Deployment

- Requires smaller datasets and can be fine-tuned for specific regions or conditions.

4. Patient-Centric Solutions

- Provides immediate feedback, reducing the time patients wait for results.

---

5. Case Studies and Success Stories

1. Detecting Pneumonia in Rural Clinics

- A small AI model deployed on portable X-ray machines achieved high accuracy in identifying pneumonia cases in rural Africa.
- **Impact**: Reduced the need to transport patients to urban hospitals for diagnosis.

2. Smartphone-Based Malaria Detection

- An app using small AI models analyzed blood smear images to detect malaria with high accuracy.
- **Impact**: Enabled quick diagnosis and treatment in regions without lab facilities.

3. Maternal Health Monitoring

- Wearable devices powered by small AI models monitored vital signs of pregnant women in rural India.
- **Impact**: Identified high-risk pregnancies, allowing timely interventions.

---

6. Challenges and Mitigation Strategies

1. Data Quality and Availability

- Limited access to high-quality medical datasets for training models.
  Solution: Collaborate with local healthcare providers to collect and annotate data.

2. Ethical Concerns

- Ensuring patient privacy and avoiding biases in diagnostics.
  Solution: Implement strict data encryption and model auditing practices.

3. Integration with Existing Systems

- Difficulty in integrating small AI models with legacy healthcare systems.
  Solution: Develop modular solutions that can work alongside existing tools.

4. Acceptance by Healthcare Workers

- Resistance to adopting AI-based tools due to lack of trust or training.
  Solution: Conduct training sessions and demonstrate model reliability to build confidence.

---

7. Future Trends and Innovations

1. Federated Learning

- Training models across decentralized devices to improve performance while preserving data privacy.

2. Multi-Modal Diagnostics

- Combining text, image, and sensor data for more comprehensive analysis.

3. Solar-Powered Diagnostics

- Deploying AI-powered devices with solar energy

solutions for off-grid locations.

4. Community-Driven AI Development

- Involving local healthcare providers in model design and testing to ensure cultural and contextual relevance.

Conclusion

Small AI models are reshaping the landscape of healthcare diagnostics in low-resource settings by providing cost-effective, portable, and accurate solutions. By addressing infrastructure challenges and enabling early detection and treatment, these models are not just enhancing healthcare accessibility but also saving lives. Their continued evolution and deployment have the potential to bridge the gap in global healthcare equity, ensuring that even the most underserved regions have access to quality diagnostics.

HEALTHCARE INNOVATIONS WITH SMALL AI MODELS: APPLICATIONS IN DRUG DEVELOPMENT

Drug development is a complex, resource-intensive process that typically spans years and requires significant financial investment. The introduction of small AI models is transforming this landscape by offering efficient, cost-effective, and scalable solutions. These models are playing a critical role in accelerating drug discovery, optimizing clinical trials, and personalizing treatment plans, making modern drug development more accessible and innovative.

---

1. Challenges in Traditional Drug Development

1. High Costs and Long Timelines

- Developing a single drug can cost billions of dollars and take 10–15 years.

2. Complexity of Biological Systems

- Understanding disease mechanisms and their interaction with potential drugs is a significant challenge.

3. Limited Data Utilization

- Underutilization of vast datasets from clinical trials and research papers due to their complexity.

4. Ethical and Regulatory Hurdles

- Stringent regulatory requirements add delays and costs.

---

2. Role of Small AI Models in Drug Development

Small AI models excel in handling specific, targeted tasks in drug development, especially in low-resource environments or situations requiring real-time processing.

1. Data Analysis and Preprocessing

- Efficiently analyzing structured and unstructured biological data.
- **Example**: Mining research papers to identify potential drug targets.

2. Predictive Modeling

- Simulating the interaction of molecules with target proteins to predict drug efficacy.
- **Example**: Identifying lead compounds in the early stages of drug discovery.

3. Real-Time Collaboration

- Supporting interdisciplinary teams with quick insights and recommendations.
- **Example**: Generating hypotheses during collaborative research sessions.

4. Running on Limited Hardware

- Their low computational requirements make them accessible in labs with constrained resources.

---

3. Key Applications of Small AI Models in Drug Development

1. Drug Discovery

- Screening millions of compounds to identify potential candidates for a specific disease.
- **Example**: Predicting molecule activity using small models trained on chemical properties and prior research.

2. Target Identification

- Identifying disease-causing genes or proteins that can be targeted with drugs.
- **Example**: Analyzing genomic datasets to find biomarkers for cancer.

3. Drug Repurposing

- Finding new applications for existing drugs by predicting off-target effects.
- **Example**: Identifying drugs for rare diseases by analyzing similarities in biological pathways.

4. Optimizing Clinical Trials

- Predicting patient responses to drugs, enabling personalized trials.
- **Example**: Segmenting patient populations to identify those most likely to benefit from a treatment.

5. Toxicology and Safety Prediction

- Predicting potential adverse effects of drug candidates before clinical trials.
- **Example**: Using small models to analyze historical data on drug safety.

---

4. Advantages of Using Small AI Models

1. Cost-Effective

- Requires fewer computational resources, reducing the cost of analysis.

2. Fast Iterations

- Quickly processes datasets, enabling rapid hypothesis testing and model retraining.

3. Enhanced Accessibility

- Can be deployed in academic labs and startups without access to high-end infrastructure.

4. Explainability

- Focused tasks allow for more interpretable results, aiding in regulatory compliance.

---

5. Case Studies and Real-World Examples

1. Predicting Drug-Protein Interactions

- Small AI models analyzed protein binding sites to predict interactions with new drug molecules.
- **Impact**: Reduced the time needed to shortlist potential drug candidates for Alzheimer's research.

2. Drug Repurposing for COVID-19

- Compact models were used to analyze existing antiviral drugs for efficacy against COVID-19.
- **Impact**: Accelerated identification of potential treatments during the pandemic.

3. Identifying Rare Disease Treatments

- Small models processed genomic data to identify potential drugs for a rare genetic disorder.
- **Impact**: Enabled targeted research into treatments for underserved conditions.

---

6. Challenges and Mitigation Strategies

1. Limited Training Data

- Small models may struggle with limited access to

high-quality data for training.
Solution: Use transfer learning and synthetic data generation to augment datasets.

2. Scalability Issues

- Handling large datasets or highly complex problems may exceed the capabilities of small models.
Solution: Combine small models with cloud-based infrastructure for hybrid scalability.

3. Bias and Errors

- Potential biases in training data can lead to inaccurate predictions.
Solution: Implement robust validation protocols and monitor for bias in predictions.

4. Regulatory Acceptance

- Convincing regulatory bodies to accept results derived from small AI models.
Solution: Emphasize transparency and provide detailed explainability for model decisions.

---

7. Future Directions and Innovations

1. Integration with High-Throughput Screening

- Combining small AI models with automated lab equipment to accelerate drug screening.

2. AI-Driven Personalized Medicine

- Using small models to tailor treatments to individual patient profiles.

3. AI for Synthetic Biology

- Designing new molecules or biological pathways with compact AI models.

4. Collaboration with Open-Source Communities

- Leveraging open-source AI frameworks to

democratize drug discovery.

Conclusion

Small AI models are reshaping drug development by making it more efficient, accessible, and data-driven. From predicting drug efficacy to optimizing clinical trials, their targeted capabilities address critical bottlenecks in the traditional process. As the technology continues to evolve, small AI models have the potential to democratize drug development, fostering innovation and delivering life-saving treatments to patients faster and more affordably.

HEALTHCARE INNOVATIONS WITH SMALL AI MODELS: LANGUAGE MODELS FOR PATIENT SUPPORT

Small AI language models are emerging as transformative tools in healthcare, particularly in patient support. These models enable personalized, efficient, and scalable communication between healthcare providers and patients, addressing common challenges such as access to information, language barriers, and timely guidance. By leveraging compact AI solutions, healthcare systems can deliver high-quality support in a cost-effective manner, even in resource-constrained settings.

---

1. The Role of Language Models in Patient Support

Language models are designed to process and generate human-like text, enabling natural interactions with patients. Their applications in patient support focus on providing accurate, empathetic, and context-aware assistance.

Key Functions:

- Answering patient queries about symptoms, medications, and procedures.
- Offering mental health support through conversational AI.
- Assisting in appointment scheduling and follow-ups.
- Translating medical advice into multiple languages for diverse populations.

---

2. Benefits of Small AI Models for Patient Support

1. Cost-Effective Deployment

- Small models require minimal computational resources, making them ideal for integration into low-cost systems, mobile apps, and telehealth platforms.

2. Accessibility

- Easily deployed on devices like smartphones, enabling access in remote or underprivileged areas.

3. Multilingual Capabilities

- Effective in breaking language barriers, providing support in regional languages or dialects.

4. Real-Time Assistance

- Delivers instant responses to patient queries, reducing the workload on human support staff.

5. Enhanced Privacy

- Smaller models can be implemented locally, ensuring sensitive patient data remains on the device.

---

3. Applications of Language Models in Patient Support

1. Symptom Checkers

- Provide patients with preliminary advice based on their symptoms.

- **Example**: Offering next-step guidance like consulting a specialist or visiting the emergency room.

2. Medication Guidance

- Educates patients on proper medication usage, potential side effects, and interactions.
- **Example**: Explaining dosage instructions for complex treatment regimens.

3. Appointment and Follow-Up Management

- Automates appointment scheduling and sends reminders to patients.
- **Example**: Rescheduling canceled appointments or alerting patients about test results.

4. Mental Health Support

- Offers initial mental health assistance through chatbots capable of empathetic communication.
- **Example**: Providing relaxation techniques or connecting users to therapists.

5. Post-Surgical Care Guidance

- Supports recovery by delivering personalized post-surgical instructions and tips.
- **Example**: Daily reminders for physiotherapy exercises or wound care.

---

4. Challenges in Implementing Small Language Models for Patient Support

1. Ensuring Accuracy

- Misinterpretation of medical data can lead to incorrect advice.
  Solution: Validate models rigorously using clinical data and expert reviews.

2. Maintaining Empathy

- AI interactions can sometimes feel impersonal.
  Solution: Train models to use empathetic language and incorporate patient feedback.

3. Handling Ambiguity in Patient Queries

- Patients may use non-medical terms or incomplete descriptions.
  Solution: Employ techniques like entity recognition and context inference to interpret queries.

4. Data Privacy Concerns

- Sensitive health data must be protected from misuse.
  Solution: Use on-device models or implement robust encryption for cloud-based solutions.

---

5. Case Studies and Real-World Implementations

1. Chatbots for Primary Care

- **Example**: An app integrating a small language model answers basic health queries and guides patients to the appropriate specialist.
- **Impact**: Reduced the burden on call centers by 40%.

2. Multilingual Support in Telemedicine

- **Example**: A rural clinic uses a small model for translating doctors' advice into local dialects.
- **Impact**: Improved patient understanding and compliance with treatments.

3. Mental Health Counseling Support

- **Example**: Compact AI-driven bots offering conversational support for individuals experiencing mild anxiety or stress.
- **Impact**: Provided accessible mental health resources to 10,000 users in underserved areas.

---

6. Future Prospects

1. Integration with Wearable Devices

- Small models can process health metrics in real time to provide personalized advice.

2. Specialized Healthcare Assistants

- Development of models tailored to specific conditions, such as diabetes or heart disease.

3. Voice-Enabled Patient Support

- Incorporating small models into voice assistants for hands-free operation.

4. Decentralized Health Applications

- Leveraging small models in edge computing environments for localized patient care.

Conclusion

Small language models are revolutionizing patient support by bridging communication gaps and making healthcare more accessible and efficient. As the technology evolves, these models have the potential to offer even more personalized, empathetic, and reliable assistance, transforming the patient experience and enhancing the overall efficiency of healthcare systems.

SMART DEVICES AND EDGE AI: VOICE ASSISTANTS IN IOT ECOSYSTEMS

The integration of voice assistants with Internet of Things (IoT) ecosystems is a pivotal development in the realm of smart devices. Voice assistants, powered by Edge AI, enable intuitive, hands-free control over a wide range of connected devices, creating a seamless and interactive user experience. These innovations are transforming how we interact with our homes, workplaces, and even healthcare environments by allowing users to control IoT devices through simple voice commands, while ensuring faster, more efficient, and localized processing of data.

---

1. The Rise of Voice Assistants in IoT

Voice assistants like Amazon's Alexa, Google Assistant, and Apple's Siri have become integral to many IoT ecosystems. As IoT devices proliferate in homes, industries, and healthcare settings, voice assistants have gained popularity as the most convenient interface for controlling and interacting with these devices. The shift towards Edge AI further enhances their functionality by enabling voice commands to be processed locally, without the need for a continuous internet connection.

Key Benefits:

- **Hands-Free Control**: Facilitates effortless interaction with connected devices.
- **Personalized Experiences**: Learns user preferences for more accurate responses and actions.
- **Scalability**: Easily integrates with a wide array of IoT devices, ranging from home appliances to security systems.

---

2. Voice Assistants and Edge AI: The Power of Localized Processing

Edge AI refers to the practice of processing data locally on devices, rather than relying on cloud-based servers. This is particularly beneficial for voice assistants integrated within IoT ecosystems, as it reduces latency, enhances data privacy, and ensures quicker responses.

Benefits of Edge AI for Voice Assistants in IoT:

- **Reduced Latency**: Voice commands are processed locally, providing real-time responses with minimal delay.
- **Enhanced Privacy**: By keeping data processing on the device, sensitive user data does not need to be transmitted to the cloud, ensuring greater privacy.
- **Improved Reliability**: In areas with limited internet connectivity, voice assistants can still function effectively as they don't require a continuous connection to the cloud.

---

3. Key Applications of Voice Assistants in IoT Ecosystems

Voice assistants powered by Edge AI are being deployed across various IoT applications, enhancing efficiency, control, and automation. Here are some of the most prominent use cases:

1. Smart Homes

- **Home Automation**: Voice assistants can control lights, thermostats, locks, and entertainment systems.
- **Example**: "Hey Google, turn off the lights" or "Alexa, adjust the temperature to 72°F."
- **Impact**: Provides convenience and energy savings by automating home devices based on voice commands.

2. Healthcare and Elderly Care

- **Medical Assistance**: In healthcare settings, voice assistants help patients manage appointments, set medication reminders, or ask health-related queries.
- **Example**: "Siri, remind me to take my blood pressure medication."
- **Impact**: Improves patient compliance and provides accessible healthcare support, particularly for elderly or disabled individuals.

3. Industrial IoT (IIoT)

- **Industrial Automation**: In manufacturing or logistics, voice assistants control machines, track inventory, and monitor systems.
- **Example**: "Alexa, start the conveyor belt" or "Hey Siri, what's the temperature in the control room?"
- **Impact**: Reduces the need for manual labor, enhancing productivity and safety in industrial environments.

4. Smart Vehicles

- **In-Car Assistance**: Voice assistants are integrated into cars to provide navigation, media control, and system settings.
- **Example**: "Hey Siri, play my workout playlist" or

"Google, find the nearest gas station."

- **Impact**: Improves driver safety by reducing distractions and enabling hands-free control of vehicle features.

---

4. Technical Foundations: Voice Recognition and Natural Language Processing (NLP)

Voice assistants in IoT ecosystems rely on advanced speech recognition algorithms and natural language processing (NLP) models. These technologies allow the voice assistants to understand and interpret user commands, even in noisy environments.

Core Components:

- **Speech Recognition**: Converts spoken words into text for interpretation. This involves feature extraction, acoustic modeling, and pattern matching.
- **Natural Language Understanding (NLU)**: Interprets the meaning behind the spoken words, enabling the assistant to comprehend user intent and context.
- **Response Generation**: Once the assistant understands the command, it uses pre-programmed rules or AI models to generate an appropriate response or action.

Edge AI Advantage:

- By embedding these processing capabilities directly into the devices (e.g., smart speakers, security cameras), edge AI reduces the need for cloud computing, ensuring faster and more accurate responses.

---

5. The Role of Edge AI in Enhancing Voice Assistants' Capabilities

Edge AI enables voice assistants to function more efficiently and autonomously. Here's how edge AI specifically benefits voice assistants in IoT ecosystems:

1. Faster Responses

- **How It Works**: Processing commands locally means that voice assistants can understand and execute requests almost instantly, without relying on a cloud connection.
- **Example**: Turning on a light or adjusting the thermostat in real-time.

2. Reduced Bandwidth Requirements

- **How It Works**: Since the voice processing is done on the device, only the essential data (such as commands or outputs) need to be sent to the cloud, reducing the strain on network bandwidth.
- **Example**: Lower latency for command execution in remote or low-bandwidth areas.

3. Increased Privacy and Security

- **How It Works**: Data, including voice commands and interactions, are processed on the device rather than being transmitted to the cloud, enhancing privacy.
- **Example**: Personal information (such as medical queries or home routines) is not sent to external servers.

4. Customization and Learning

- **How It Works**: Small AI models running on the device can adapt to user preferences over time, providing a more personalized experience.
- **Example**: Voice assistants can learn users' patterns, like preferred room temperatures or favorite music genres.

---

6. Future Trends and Innovations

The role of voice assistants in IoT ecosystems will continue to evolve with advancements in AI and machine learning. Key trends to watch for include:

1. Increased Integration with Smart Devices

- Voice assistants will control an even wider range of IoT devices, including wearables, appliances, and even IoT-enabled medical devices.

2. Multi-Modal Interactions

- Future voice assistants will combine voice with other forms of input (e.g., gestures, facial recognition, or touch), enabling a more intuitive and seamless user experience.

3. Enhanced Security and Authentication

- Voice assistants will incorporate advanced voice biometrics for secure, hands-free authentication in sensitive environments like banking or healthcare.

4. Advanced Natural Language Understanding

- Future models will better understand context, emotions, and nuances, allowing for more natural, human-like conversations.

---

7. Conclusion

Voice assistants powered by Edge AI are transforming IoT ecosystems by making them more accessible, efficient, and secure. Their ability to process commands locally ensures faster, more reliable responses, with the added benefit of enhancing privacy and reducing bandwidth dependency. As the technology advances, voice assistants will become an even more integral part of our everyday lives, from managing smart homes to supporting healthcare systems and industrial automation. By leveraging small, efficient AI models at the edge, voice assistants will continue to drive innovation across various sectors, paving the way for more intelligent and responsive IoT environments.

SMART DEVICES AND EDGE AI: AI FOR WEARABLE DEVICES

Wearable devices are revolutionizing various aspects of our daily lives, from health and fitness tracking to real-time communication and entertainment. The integration of Artificial Intelligence (AI) with wearable devices, particularly when powered by Edge AI, is unlocking new capabilities, enabling enhanced functionality, and improving user experience. Edge AI allows for faster processing and reduced reliance on cloud infrastructure, making wearable devices more efficient, responsive, and secure.

---

1. The Rise of Wearable Devices and AI Integration

Wearable devices, such as smartwatches, fitness trackers, health monitors, and augmented reality (AR) glasses, are gaining popularity due to their convenience and ability to provide real-time data and insights. These devices are designed to be worn continuously, offering a seamless experience and real-time interaction. When combined with AI, these devices can process data more intelligently, adapting to individual needs and providing personalized experiences.

Key Benefits of AI in Wearables:

- **Personalization**: Wearable devices can track and analyze users' behaviors, adapting recommendations and feedback to improve their health, fitness, or productivity.

- **Real-Time Analytics**: AI algorithms can analyze data from sensors and provide immediate insights, such as monitoring heart rate, sleep patterns, or detecting potential health risks.
- **Autonomous Decision-Making**: AI enables wearables to make real-time decisions based on environmental inputs, user activity, or health data, such as alerting users to dangerous situations (e.g., heart attack detection).

---

2. The Role of Edge AI in Wearable Devices

Edge AI refers to the processing of data locally on the device, rather than relying on a central server or cloud system. This has significant advantages for wearable devices, as it allows for real-time data analysis, reduced latency, and enhanced privacy.

Benefits of Edge AI for Wearables:

- **Faster Response Times**: Since the data is processed locally, decisions can be made in real time without the need for external communication, leading to faster responses.
- **Reduced Latency**: Immediate processing allows wearables to provide instant feedback to the user, such as step count updates or heart rate monitoring.
- **Improved Privacy and Security**: Personal health data, such as activity levels and heart rate, can be kept on the device rather than transmitted to the cloud, ensuring greater security and privacy.
- **Offline Functionality**: Edge AI allows wearable devices to continue functioning even without a stable internet connection, ensuring reliable performance in remote or low-connectivity areas.

3. Key Applications of AI in Wearable Devices

Wearable devices enhanced by AI are being deployed in various industries, especially healthcare, fitness, and personal productivity. Below are some of the most prominent applications:

1. Health and Fitness Monitoring

- **Activity and Sleep Tracking**: AI algorithms in wearables track and analyze activity patterns, providing insights into daily movements, sleep quality, and overall wellness.
- **Example**: Smartwatches like the Apple Watch or Fitbit can monitor heart rate, steps, calories burned, and sleep cycles, offering personalized recommendations based on the collected data.
- **Impact**: Provides users with actionable insights to optimize their exercise routines, improve sleep quality, and maintain a healthy lifestyle.

2. Health Diagnostics and Early Detection

- **Chronic Condition Monitoring**: Wearables with integrated AI can help monitor chronic conditions, such as diabetes, hypertension, and asthma, by tracking key metrics like blood glucose levels, blood pressure, and respiratory rate.
- **Example**: AI-enabled wearables can detect irregular heart rhythms or alert users about abnormal spikes in blood pressure, helping identify potential health issues before they become critical.
- **Impact**: Enables proactive healthcare by providing early warnings and reducing hospital visits through continuous monitoring.

3. Stress and Mental Health Monitoring

- **Emotion Recognition**: AI can analyze physiological data (such as heart rate variability) to detect signs of stress or emotional distress, allowing wearables to suggest relaxation techniques or mindfulness exercises.
- **Example**: Devices like the Oura Ring or smartwatches can alert users when they are experiencing elevated stress levels and suggest activities like breathing exercises or meditation.
- **Impact**: Promotes mental well-being by encouraging users to manage stress in real-time.

4. Fitness Coaching and Personalized Recommendations

- **AI-Driven Fitness Plans**: Wearables can analyze user activity and recommend personalized workout routines to help individuals achieve specific fitness goals, such as weight loss, muscle gain, or endurance improvement.
- **Example**: Wearables with AI capabilities can dynamically adjust fitness plans based on real-time performance metrics, tailoring workouts to match users' progress and goals.
- **Impact**: Encourages more effective training and helps users achieve long-term fitness results.

---

4. AI and Machine Learning Models in Wearables

AI algorithms and machine learning (ML) models are at the heart of wearable devices, helping them process data, recognize patterns, and make intelligent decisions.

Key AI Techniques Used in Wearables:

- **Supervised Learning**: Algorithms are trained on labeled datasets to recognize specific patterns in health or activity data, such as identifying abnormal heart rhythms or classifying types of physical exercises.

- **Unsupervised Learning**: AI models can identify hidden patterns in user behavior without labeled data, allowing wearables to adapt to individual habits and preferences.
- **Reinforcement Learning**: AI can use reinforcement learning to continuously adjust recommendations based on user feedback and engagement. For instance, suggesting improvements in a workout routine based on past performance and results.

---

5. The Future of AI-Powered Wearables

As wearable technology continues to evolve, AI will play an even more significant role in enhancing their capabilities. Future trends and innovations in wearable AI include:

1. Biometric Authentication and Security

- Wearables will use AI-driven biometric sensors (such as heart rate or voice recognition) to authenticate users, offering a secure and convenient way to access devices and apps.

2. Advanced Health Diagnostics

- The future of wearables may include more advanced health monitoring, including the ability to predict medical conditions such as strokes, seizures, or sleep apnea by analyzing real-time physiological data.

3. Real-Time Environmental Interaction

- Wearables will be able to analyze environmental data (such as temperature, humidity, or pollution levels) and provide real-time feedback, helping users adapt to changing conditions. For example, a wearable might alert users about unhealthy air quality or recommend appropriate clothing for the weather.

4. Integration with Smart Cities

- Wearables could become integrated with smart city infrastructure, allowing them to communicate with public systems, such as traffic lights or health services, to provide real-time updates on traffic conditions, environmental factors, or emergency alerts.

---

6. Conclusion

AI and Edge AI are transforming wearable devices, enabling them to provide more intelligent, real-time, and personalized experiences. By processing data locally on the device, these wearables offer faster response times, improved privacy, and the ability to function even in remote environments. From fitness and health monitoring to mental wellness and stress management, AI-powered wearables are revolutionizing the way we track and improve our health. As technology continues to advance, wearables will play an even more pivotal role in enhancing our daily lives and ensuring proactive healthcare, making them an essential tool for personal well-being and productivity.

SMART DEVICES AND EDGE AI: REAL-TIME LANGUAGE MODELS ON MOBILE DEVICES

The proliferation of smart devices and mobile phones has fundamentally transformed how we interact with technology. With the rise of Edge AI and real-time language models, mobile devices are now capable of offering advanced natural language processing (NLP) capabilities, enabling seamless, intelligent interactions without relying on cloud-based systems. By performing computations locally on the device, Edge AI ensures faster, more responsive, and secure experiences. Real-time language models on mobile devices empower users to engage with technology in more natural and intuitive ways.

---

1. The Evolution of Real-Time Language Models in Mobile Devices

Mobile devices have traditionally relied on cloud-based servers to process complex language tasks. However, as hardware capabilities of smartphones and tablets continue to improve, there has been a significant shift toward Edge AI. With small, optimized models running locally on the device, mobile phones are now able to understand and generate natural language in real-time, enabling instant communication, voice recognition, and automated translation.

Key Trends Driving Real-Time Language Models on Mobile:

- **Advancements in Mobile Hardware**: Modern smartphones are equipped with powerful processors, GPUs, and dedicated AI chips, allowing for the processing of AI models directly on the device.
- **Improved Model Optimization**: Techniques such as model pruning, quantization, and distillation allow language models to be compressed while maintaining performance, making them suitable for mobile deployment.
- **5G Connectivity**: With the advent of 5G, real-time language models on mobile devices can benefit from faster network speeds and reduced latency, further enhancing the user experience.

---

2. Key Benefits of Real-Time Language Models on Mobile Devices

Real-time language models powered by Edge AI offer several advantages, especially in terms of speed, privacy, and accessibility:

1. Low Latency and Fast Responses

- **Real-Time Interactions**: By processing data locally, mobile devices can generate responses to voice commands, text input, or queries instantly, reducing the delay that would otherwise be caused by cloud communication.
- **Example**: Voice assistants like Siri, Google Assistant, and Alexa, powered by real-time language models, can instantly process and respond to queries without the need for round-trip communication to a cloud server.

2. Enhanced Privacy and Data Security

- **Local Data Processing**: With language models

running on the device, personal data such as voice commands, messages, and user interactions are processed locally, ensuring better privacy and reducing the risk of data breaches.

- **Example**: When dictating a message or searching for a sensitive query, the data stays on the device, preventing potential eavesdropping or unauthorized access from third-party servers.

3. Offline Functionality

- **Autonomous Performance Without Connectivity**: Mobile devices can perform language-based tasks without relying on an internet connection, making them ideal for areas with poor or no network access.
- **Example**: In regions with limited connectivity, voice-to-text and language translation can be performed offline, allowing users to use language models when traveling or in remote locations.

4. Reduced Dependence on Cloud Infrastructure

- **Decreased Cloud Dependency**: Running language models on mobile devices reduces the strain on cloud servers and ensures the device operates independently without constant communication with the cloud.
- **Example**: Translation apps, for instance, can provide real-time translations directly on the device, without sending data back and forth to a server for processing.

---

3. Applications of Real-Time Language Models on Mobile Devices

The integration of real-time language models on mobile devices opens up a wide array of possibilities across multiple domains, from personal productivity to entertainment and global communication.

1. Voice Assistants and Virtual Assistants

- **Voice Interaction**: Real-time language models allow users to interact with their devices using natural language commands. Voice assistants can perform tasks such as setting reminders, answering questions, or controlling smart home devices.
- **Example**: Apple's Siri, Google Assistant, and Amazon Alexa all rely on real-time language models to interpret and respond to user commands instantly.
- **Impact**: This enhances user experience by providing more intuitive, hands-free, and efficient interaction with devices.

2. Real-Time Translation

- **Language Translation**: Mobile devices can leverage real-time language models to provide instant translations between languages, making communication smoother in multilingual environments.
- **Example**: Apps like Google Translate and iTranslate can translate text or speech on the fly, without requiring an internet connection, using compact language models optimized for mobile devices.
- **Impact**: Enables cross-cultural communication, supports travelers, and enhances language learning by providing immediate feedback.

3. Text Generation and Editing

- **Content Creation**: Real-time language models on mobile devices can assist in writing, editing, and generating content, including emails, documents, or social media posts.
- **Example**: Apps like Grammarly and Microsoft Word

use AI to check grammar, suggest improvements, and even generate sentences or paragraphs based on input.

- **Impact**: Boosts productivity by automating writing tasks and improving the quality of text on-the-go.

4. Sentiment Analysis and Emotion Recognition

- **Sentiment Detection**: Mobile apps equipped with real-time language models can analyze user input, such as text messages or reviews, to determine the sentiment behind the content (e.g., positive, negative, neutral).
- **Example**: Social media platforms and customer service apps use sentiment analysis to gauge user feedback, ensuring timely responses and targeted actions.
- **Impact**: Provides businesses with insights into customer satisfaction and helps personalize user experiences based on emotional context.

5. Speech-to-Text and Dictation

- **Real-Time Transcription**: Real-time language models enable mobile devices to convert speech into text instantly, improving accessibility for people with hearing impairments and providing efficient dictation for productivity.
- **Example**: Smartphones and virtual assistants can transcribe spoken words to text in real-time, making them ideal for note-taking, meeting transcription, and hands-free writing.
- **Impact**: Enhances accessibility, boosts productivity, and enables multitasking.

---

4. Challenges of Real-Time Language Models on Mobile Devices

While the integration of real-time language models on mobile devices offers several benefits, it also comes with its own set of challenges that need to be addressed for further advancement:

1. Computational Limitations

- **Hardware Constraints**: Mobile devices, while powerful, still have limited computational resources compared to cloud-based servers. Real-time language models must be highly optimized to run efficiently on these devices without consuming too much power or memory.

2. Battery Consumption

- **Power Consumption**: Running complex language models continuously can drain the battery of mobile devices, posing a challenge for developers to balance performance with power efficiency.

3. Model Optimization

- **Compression and Accuracy**: One of the biggest challenges is compressing large language models to fit on mobile devices without compromising performance. Striking the right balance between model size, processing speed, and accuracy is essential for a seamless user experience.

---

5. The Future of Real-Time Language Models on Mobile Devices

As hardware and software technology continue to advance, the future of real-time language models on mobile devices looks promising. With the evolution of AI chips, faster processors, and improved optimization techniques, we can expect mobile devices to support more powerful language models capable of handling more complex tasks.

Future Innovations in Mobile AI:

- **Enhanced Personalization**: Real-time models will

learn and adapt to user behavior more effectively, offering highly personalized experiences tailored to individual preferences, interests, and daily routines.

- **Multilingual and Cross-Cultural Capabilities**: AI models will be able to offer more seamless and accurate real-time translation services, breaking down language barriers and enabling global communication.
- **Context-Aware AI**: Real-time language models will become more context-aware, considering user location, activity, and environment to provide more relevant and timely responses.

---

6. Conclusion

Real-time language models on mobile devices, powered by Edge AI, are transforming the way users interact with their smartphones, wearables, and other smart devices. With the ability to process language data locally, mobile devices can provide faster, more secure, and offline-capable language services that improve user experience and accessibility. As AI and mobile technologies continue to evolve, the potential for more advanced, context-aware, and personalized language models will only increase, further enhancing the capabilities of smart devices across various applications.

LANGUAGE MODELS FOR LOW-RESOURCE AND REGIONAL LANGUAGES: BRIDGING LANGUAGE GAPS IN EMERGING ECONOMIES

The rapid growth of natural language processing (NLP) technologies has revolutionized how we interact with machines, but a significant gap remains in the availability of language resources for low-resource and regional languages. These languages, spoken by millions of people in emerging economies, often lack sufficient digital content and trained AI models to ensure accessibility and support for essential services. However, compact AI models, along with advancements in language modeling techniques, are now bridging these gaps, making AI-powered language services more inclusive.

---

1. The Need for Language Models in Low-Resource and Regional Languages

In emerging economies, many languages are either underrepresented in digital form or lack large-scale datasets necessary for training robust language models. Despite this, these languages are vital to the cultural identity and daily lives of millions of people. The absence of AI-powered services for these languages has led to digital exclusion, where speakers of these languages are unable to access key services such as healthcare, education, customer support, and governmental resources in their native tongue.

Challenges:

- **Limited Digital Resources**: Many low-resource languages have little to no digital presence, lacking content such as books, news, or even social media posts to build large, diverse language corpora.
- **Data Scarcity**: High-quality, annotated datasets for these languages are often scarce, making training high-performance models more challenging.
- **Linguistic Diversity**: Regional languages may have diverse dialects and variations, further complicating the development of unified language models.

---

2. Bridging the Gap: The Role of Compact AI Models

Compact AI models offer a promising solution to the challenges posed by low-resource languages. These models are optimized to run on devices with limited computational power while still delivering high performance. When applied to low-resource languages, they can democratize access to advanced language technologies, even in economically disadvantaged regions.

How Compact AI Models Help:

- **Model Efficiency**: Compact models use fewer resources while maintaining reasonable accuracy. Techniques such as distillation, quantization, and pruning allow models to perform well even with smaller, lower-quality datasets.

- **Localized Training**: Small language models can be trained on locally available datasets, meaning that even with limited digital content, they can provide valuable language processing services tailored to specific regions or dialects.
- **Adaptability**: Compact models can be fine-tuned on diverse linguistic data, helping them adapt to different regional dialects or specific cultural contexts.

---

3. Techniques for Developing Language Models for Low-Resource Languages

Several advanced techniques are now being employed to create robust language models for low-resource and regional languages. These techniques allow researchers to maximize the utility of small datasets and limited computational resources.

1. Transfer Learning and Multilingual Models

- **Transfer Learning**: By using large pre-trained models in high-resource languages (like English or Mandarin), researchers can transfer learned knowledge to smaller models for underrepresented languages. This allows for faster and more efficient training with fewer resources.
- **Multilingual Models**: Models like mBERT and XLM-R are designed to work across multiple languages. These models can be fine-tuned to perform well even on languages with limited digital data by leveraging shared linguistic features across languages.

2. Data Augmentation

- **Synthetic Data Generation**: Techniques such as

back-translation (translating content back and forth between languages) or generating synthetic sentences can augment small datasets, increasing the variety and volume of language data available for training.

- **Crowdsourcing**: Involving native speakers to annotate data, translate text, or generate language content can help in collecting diverse data for underrepresented languages.

3. Zero-Shot Learning

- **Zero-Shot Models**: Zero-shot learning allows a language model to perform tasks on a language it has never been directly trained on. By leveraging universal linguistic features, these models can apply learned knowledge from high-resource languages to predict text or classify speech in low-resource languages.

4. Low-Resource Fine-Tuning

- **Fine-Tuning Pretrained Models**: Even when limited data is available, fine-tuning a pretrained model (such as a multilingual or cross-lingual model) on specific low-resource language datasets can result in significant improvements in language understanding and processing.

---

4. Real-World Applications in Emerging Economies

Compact AI models for low-resource and regional languages are already making a significant impact in a range of practical applications, improving access to essential services for millions of people in emerging economies.

1. Healthcare Access

- **Language Models for Health Communication**: Compact AI models are enabling healthcare services to communicate with patients in their native languages, making medical advice, appointments, and information more accessible. For example, language models can power chatbots or virtual assistants that help people navigate health systems in low-resource languages.

- **Example**: In India, local language models are helping people with rural backgrounds understand health-related information, receive diagnoses, or follow up on treatment through mobile apps and digital platforms.

2. Education and Literacy

- **E-Learning and Education**: By leveraging language models that support regional languages, educational platforms can provide tailored content in languages spoken by students. This makes education more inclusive, reaching children in rural and remote areas who speak regional languages that are not widely used in traditional academic settings.
- **Example**: In Africa, mobile applications that teach literacy in local languages are empowering students in regions with limited access to quality education, allowing them to learn and engage with educational content in their own language.

3. Customer Support and E-Government Services

- **Automated Customer Support**: Businesses and government agencies are increasingly using AI-driven chatbots to provide 24/7 support in regional languages. This helps address customer queries, process requests, and provide information, all in a language that users understand.
- **Example**: In Latin America, small language models are enabling customer service in Spanish,

Portuguese, and indigenous languages, helping companies and governments interact with a broader range of citizens.

4. Voice Assistants for Regional Languages

- **Voice Interaction in Local Languages**: Compact AI models are facilitating the development of voice assistants that can understand and respond to voice commands in regional languages, significantly improving usability in rural or underserved areas.
- **Example**: In Southeast Asia, voice assistants in regional dialects are transforming how people interact with mobile phones, making it easier for individuals who are not fluent in English to use smartphones for a variety of tasks, from setting reminders to asking for directions.

---

5. Overcoming Challenges in Low-Resource Language Modeling

Despite the progress made, several challenges remain in developing effective language models for low-resource languages:

1. Dialectal Variations

- **Managing Dialects**: Many regional languages have numerous dialects, making it difficult for models to generalize effectively. For example, a language model trained on Hindi may perform poorly with dialects like Awadhi or Bhojpuri.
- **Solution**: Collaborative efforts involving local linguists and native speakers are needed to create comprehensive datasets that include various dialects and linguistic nuances.

2. Data Scarcity

- **Lack of Annotated Data**: Annotated corpora for low-resource languages are often lacking, which hinders model development.

- **Solution**: Crowdsourcing and partnerships with local universities and research institutions can help overcome data limitations.

3. Resource Constraints

- **Limited Infrastructure**: Many emerging economies may lack the computational resources to train large models or deploy them on mobile devices.
- **Solution**: Compact, optimized models that require fewer resources are an effective way to address these infrastructure limitations.

---

6. The Future of Language Models for Low-Resource Languages

The future of AI-powered language models for low-resource languages looks promising. As technology continues to evolve, new techniques for model optimization, data collection, and community-driven research will enable even greater inclusivity and accessibility for regional languages.

Key Trends to Watch:

- **Increased Collaboration**: Collaboration between researchers, governments, and local communities will help collect diverse data and build more inclusive AI systems.
- **AI for Digital Inclusion**: Compact language models will continue to drive digital inclusion by providing essential services in regional languages, allowing people in emerging economies to benefit from AI technologies.
- **Voice Technology Expansion**: The growth of voice-based interfaces will make AI services even more accessible, especially for people with limited literacy.

7. Conclusion

Language models for low-resource and regional languages are essential for bridging the digital divide in emerging economies. With the help of compact AI models, we can unlock new opportunities for millions of people who speak languages that are often left behind in the digital revolution. By continuing to invest in research, technology, and local data collection, AI can provide powerful tools for education, healthcare, and communication in the languages that matter most to people around the world.

LANGUAGE MODELS FOR LOW-RESOURCE AND REGIONAL LANGUAGES: CHALLENGES IN DEVELOPING LOW-RESOURCE LANGUAGE MODELS

Developing effective language models for low-resource and regional languages presents numerous challenges that arise from linguistic, technological, and societal factors. These challenges make it difficult to create robust, accurate, and scalable AI models that can cater to the unique needs of speakers in these regions. Despite the growing importance of AI-powered language technologies, many languages spoken by millions of people around the world are still underserved due to these challenges. In this section, we will explore the primary obstacles to developing language models for low-resource and regional languages.

1. Data Scarcity

Challenges:

- **Limited Digital Data**: Low-resource languages often lack sufficient digital content like books, articles, social media posts, and other textual data that is needed to train large language models. As a result, there is a significant gap in the availability of language corpora for these languages.
- **Lack of Annotated Datasets**: Even when digital content exists, it may not be annotated (labeled or structured) for specific tasks like sentiment analysis or named entity recognition, which are crucial for training supervised models.
- **Historical Linguistic Gaps**: For many regional languages, historical records or standardized grammar rules may not exist, limiting the scope of data collection.

Impact:

- The absence of sufficient training data can lead to poor model performance, as language models require large and diverse datasets to understand the complexities of syntax, grammar, and semantics in a given language.

Solution:

- **Crowdsourcing and Community Contributions**: Crowdsourcing data collection and annotation can help create more comprehensive datasets. Native speakers can contribute to building language resources through community-driven platforms.
- **Data Augmentation**: Techniques like back-translation, synthetic data generation, or bootstrapping from closely related languages can help supplement the available data.

---

2. Linguistic Diversity and Dialect Variations

Challenges:

- **Multiple Dialects**: Many low-resource languages have a high degree of dialectal variation. For instance, a language like Hindi has numerous dialects, each with unique lexical, phonetic, and grammatical features. A single language model might struggle to generalize across these dialects, as models tend to perform poorly if they are not trained on data that represents the full linguistic diversity.
- **Lack of Standardization**: In some languages, there is no standardized written form, and different regions might use different orthographies, spelling conventions, or vocabulary. For instance, regional variations in writing and pronunciation can lead to ambiguities that are challenging for language models to resolve.

Impact:

- Dialectal diversity can reduce the accuracy of language models and limit their ability to understand regional variations in speech and text.

Solution:

- **Dialect-Specific Models**: Creating separate models for different dialects or including a large variety of dialect data in training datasets can help address this issue.
- **Transfer Learning**: Using pre-trained multilingual models and fine-tuning them on specific dialects can help models adapt to diverse linguistic variations.

---

3. Computational Resources and Infrastructure Limitations

Challenges:

- **Lack of Infrastructure**: In many regions where low-resource languages are spoken, there is limited access to advanced computing resources and high-performance hardware. This limits the ability to train large-scale models that require significant computational power.
- **Cost of Model Training**: Training large language models requires access to powerful GPUs, large datasets, and cloud computing resources. For many regions, the financial cost of these resources can be prohibitive.

Impact:

- Without the necessary infrastructure, AI development for low-resource languages often becomes limited or delayed. The lack of local hardware capabilities can also hinder the deployment of trained models in regions with inadequate tech infrastructure.

Solution:

- **Compact and Efficient Models**: Small, efficient models can be trained with fewer computational resources and deployed on less powerful devices. Techniques such as model pruning, quantization, and distillation help to reduce the computational overhead.
- **Edge Computing and Mobile AI**: By utilizing mobile devices and edge computing, smaller language models can be run directly on local devices without relying on cloud resources, making them more accessible in low-resource settings.

---

4. Limited Linguistic Expertise and Research

Challenges:

- **Scarcity of Linguists and Researchers**: Many low-resource languages are spoken in regions where there is a shortage of researchers and linguists with the expertise required to develop high-quality AI models. These languages often lack formal linguistic studies or research on phonetics, syntax, and morphology, which are critical for building effective NLP systems.
- **Lack of Linguistic Infrastructure**: In some regions, there may not be enough linguistic infrastructure (e.g., linguistic databases, annotated corpora) to support the development of AI models. The absence of resources like dictionaries, thesauri, and grammar books makes it difficult for researchers to formalize and standardize language models.

Impact:

- Without adequate expertise, AI models may misinterpret or fail to capture the richness and diversity of low-resource languages, leading to biased or ineffective models.

Solution:

- **Collaboration with Local Linguists**: Partnering with local universities and linguistic experts can help create accurate datasets and build better models that reflect the true diversity of language usage in the region.
- **Cross-Disciplinary Research**: Collaborating with anthropologists, sociolinguists, and cultural studies experts can provide deeper insights into the language and its usage patterns, which can be crucial for building accurate models.

---

5. Cultural and Societal Factors

Challenges:

- **Cultural Sensitivity**: Low-resource and regional languages are deeply tied to the cultural contexts in which they are spoken. Language models must account for these nuances to avoid producing culturally insensitive or irrelevant results.
- **Data Bias and Representation**: Language models trained on small datasets may inherit biases from those datasets, such as gender biases, racial biases, or biases related to regional or social status. Additionally, a lack of diverse voices in the data can lead to skewed representations.
- **Language Endangerment**: Many low-resource languages are at risk of extinction, and their speakers often face social pressures to adopt dominant languages like English or Mandarin. This can create challenges in maintaining the relevance and sustainability of language models.

Impact:

- Cultural misunderstandings or biased AI outcomes can erode trust in technology. Models that do not reflect the true diversity of the people they are meant to serve are less likely to be adopted or successful.

Solution:

- **Inclusive Data Collection**: Ensuring that language models reflect the full spectrum of speakers within a community is crucial. This means incorporating data from different social groups, regions, and contexts.
- **Culturally-Aware AI**: Incorporating cultural sensitivity into language models is essential to ensure they respect and reflect local customs, traditions, and values.

---

6. Cross-Language and Cross-Cultural Transfer

Challenges:

- **Translating Knowledge Across Languages**: Transfer learning is an important method for developing language models for low-resource languages. However, the challenge lies in transferring knowledge from high-resource languages without losing the linguistic nuances specific to low-resource languages.
- **Shared Resources**: Low-resource languages often share common linguistic features with other regional languages, but these shared characteristics may not always be enough to generalize effectively.

Impact:

- The effectiveness of cross-lingual approaches may be limited if the models cannot fully understand the unique characteristics of the low-resource languages.

Solution:

- **Multilingual and Cross-Lingual Models**: Leveraging multilingual models such as mBERT (multilingual BERT) or XLM-R can enable the sharing of knowledge between languages, thus improving performance on low-resource languages.

---

7. Ethical Considerations and Privacy

Challenges:

- **Privacy Concerns**: In regions where data privacy laws are not robust, there may be concerns about the misuse of personal data for training language models. Protecting the privacy of individuals while collecting data for language model training is a critical issue.
- **Ethical AI Use**: Low-resource languages are often spoken by marginalized communities, and deploying

AI models in such regions without addressing ethical considerations can exacerbate social inequalities and perpetuate biases.

Impact:

- Failure to respect privacy or ethical standards can lead to distrust in AI systems and hinder their adoption in sensitive regions.

Solution:

- **Privacy-Preserving AI**: Implementing techniques like federated learning or differential privacy can help ensure that data used to train language models is kept private and secure.
- **Ethical Guidelines and Oversight**: Engaging local communities and stakeholders in the development of AI systems ensures that cultural sensitivities and ethical concerns are addressed.

Conclusion

Developing language models for low-resource and regional languages involves navigating a complex landscape of data limitations, linguistic diversity, technological challenges, and societal factors. Addressing these challenges requires innovative solutions, collaboration with local communities, and the use of efficient AI models that can work within the constraints of available resources. However, the potential benefits are enormous: enabling millions of speakers to access vital services, preserve their languages, and engage with the digital world in meaningful ways. With continued investment in research and technology, compact language models can help bridge the gap and foster a more inclusive AI-powered future.

LANGUAGE MODELS FOR LOW-RESOURCE AND REGIONAL LANGUAGES: CASE STUDIES: SUCCESS STORIES IN LOCALIZATION

In recent years, there have been several successful initiatives and projects that have used AI and language models to address the challenges of low-resource and regional languages. These success stories highlight the potential of technology to empower marginalized communities, preserve languages, and improve access to services. The following case studies provide insights into how compact language models are transforming the landscape of low-resource language localization.

---

1. Google Translate for African Languages

Background:

African languages have long been underrepresented in the digital world, with many lacking sufficient resources for machine translation. Google Translate's efforts to incorporate

African languages into its system have been groundbreaking.

Success Story:

- **Project Approach**: Google's approach involved using machine learning techniques to build translation models for African languages, despite the lack of large-scale, publicly available data. Google used a combination of multilingual models and data augmentation techniques to create effective models for these languages.
- **Key Achievements**:
  - Google Translate now supports over 20 African languages, such as Yoruba, Amharic, and Zulu.
  - Leveraged transfer learning and unsupervised machine translation, enabling efficient training without large datasets.
  - The introduction of these languages into Google Translate has had a direct impact on users, allowing millions to translate documents, websites, and messages in their native tongues.

Impact:

- **Cultural Preservation**: The integration of African languages in mainstream technology helps preserve these languages and make them more accessible to younger generations.
- **Digital Inclusion**: Improved access to essential services, educational resources, and communication tools for millions of speakers of African languages.

---

2. Facebook's AI Models for Indian Languages

Background:

India is home to hundreds of languages and dialects, many of which are spoken by millions but remain largely absent from digital spaces. Facebook has made significant strides in localizing its platform for Indian languages.

Success Story:

- **Project Approach**: Facebook has developed AI models for over 10 Indian languages, including Hindi, Bengali, Telugu, and Tamil. The company leveraged large multilingual transformer models and neural machine translation systems to translate posts, comments, and messages.
- **Key Achievements**:
    - AI models trained on low-resource languages using parallel data (translation datasets) and unsupervised learning methods.
    - Facebook's AI systems can now automatically translate posts, enabling users to interact in their native languages while also breaking down barriers between different linguistic communities.
    - Facebook has also created specialized language tools for Hindi and other Indian languages, allowing users to engage with posts written in regional scripts.

Impact:

- **Increased Engagement**: Users are more engaged when content is available in their native language, helping people from diverse linguistic backgrounds connect and participate more actively on the platform.
- **Bridging Linguistic Barriers**: By supporting regional languages, Facebook has made digital spaces more inclusive, facilitating access to information, education, and social interaction for speakers of these languages.

---

3. Mozilla Common Voice: Open-Source Speech Data

Collection for Regional Languages

Background:

For many low-resource languages, there is a severe lack of audio data necessary for developing speech recognition systems. Mozilla's Common Voice project is designed to address this issue by crowd-sourcing speech data.

Success Story:

- **Project Approach**: Mozilla created an open-source platform where volunteers from around the world can contribute their voices, helping build speech recognition models for a variety of languages. The platform targets both widely spoken and underrepresented languages.
- **Key Achievements**:
  - The Common Voice project now includes contributions from over 50 languages, including languages like Kannada, Welsh, and Cebuano.
  - The project provides datasets for free, enabling developers and researchers to use the data to train and improve AI-based speech systems.
  - It has successfully created speech-to-text models for languages previously excluded from modern AI tools, providing a foundation for other applications, such as voice assistants and transcription tools.

Impact:

- **Cultural and Linguistic Preservation**: By collecting and digitizing spoken data, the project helps preserve regional languages and ensures that these languages are represented in future technologies.
- **Enhanced Access to Technology**: Speech recognition models tailored for low-resource languages make

technology more accessible to people who rely on voice commands or who have limited literacy skills.

---

4. Microsoft's AI for Southeast Asian Languages

Background:

Southeast Asia is home to a diverse range of languages, many of which lack the resources for large-scale machine learning models. Microsoft has worked to localize its products and services for these languages using AI.

Success Story:

- **Project Approach**: Microsoft leveraged its existing AI infrastructure, including pre-trained language models, and fine-tuned them on data specific to Southeast Asian languages like Vietnamese, Malay, and Thai. The company also used machine translation and natural language processing (NLP) to improve the accessibility of their products for local users.
- **Key Achievements**:
    - Microsoft's efforts have led to improved translation capabilities, allowing users to access Microsoft Office products and services in their native languages.
    - Enhanced speech recognition for Thai and Vietnamese, supporting virtual assistants like Cortana and other voice-driven applications.

Impact:

- **Business Empowerment**: Southeast Asian businesses have benefited from AI-driven translations, improving the customer experience and making global communication easier.
- **Inclusive Access**: Users in the region can now access information, entertainment, and digital services in

their native languages, improving overall digital inclusion.

---

5. Indigenous Language Preservation: AI for Navajo

Background:

The Navajo language, spoken by the Navajo Nation in the United States, faces significant challenges due to its declining number of speakers and the lack of linguistic resources. AI initiatives have been developed to preserve and revitalize this Indigenous language.

Success Story:

- **Project Approach**: Google and the Navajo Nation worked together to develop a voice search tool for the Navajo language. The project utilized a small language model to train a speech-to-text system specifically for Navajo.
- **Key Achievements**:
  - Google built the first Navajo speech recognition system, allowing users to speak commands in Navajo and receive responses in the language.
  - The system has been integrated into Google Assistant, allowing speakers of the language to use their native tongue for voice searches, sending messages, and controlling smart devices.

Impact:

- **Cultural Revitalization**: The project has sparked a renewed interest in the Navajo language among younger generations, who are more likely to engage with technology in their native language.
- **Technology for Language Preservation**: The AI-driven system plays an essential role in preserving the language and making it relevant in modern

digital spaces.

---

6. Language Localization in Brazil: AI for Portuguese Dialects

Background:

Brazil is a large, diverse country where multiple dialects of Portuguese are spoken. Many of these dialects present challenges for standard AI language models, which are typically trained on European Portuguese.

Success Story:

- **Project Approach**: Brazilian tech companies and researchers have worked together to develop machine learning models that specifically address the unique linguistic features of Brazilian Portuguese dialects. This includes creating specialized models for speech recognition, sentiment analysis, and translation.
- **Key Achievements**:
  - AI-driven virtual assistants, like those on Brazilian mobile phones, have been tailored to understand Brazilian Portuguese dialects, improving user interaction.
  - Sentiment analysis and customer support systems have been localized to better understand colloquial expressions and regional vocabulary specific to Brazilian Portuguese.

Impact:

- **Enhanced Communication**: These AI systems have made it easier for Brazilian consumers to interact with digital platforms, improving their experience and accessibility.
- **Localization of Content**: Portuguese-language content, from social media posts to customer service inquiries, has become more accurate and regionally

relevant.

Conclusion

The case studies presented demonstrate the transformative potential of compact and efficient language models in addressing the challenges of low-resource and regional languages. These success stories are not only proof of concept but also inspire further innovation in the field of AI localization. By overcoming the challenges of data scarcity, linguistic diversity, and technological barriers, these projects have helped millions of people access digital services, preserve their cultures, and participate more fully in the digital world. The continued success of such initiatives will contribute to a more inclusive and linguistically diverse AI ecosystem.

ENVIRONMENTAL AND ETHICAL PERSPECTIVES: ENERGY EFFICIENCY IN COMPACT MODELS

As artificial intelligence (AI) continues to evolve, the environmental and ethical implications of deploying AI technologies become increasingly important. In particular, compact models, which offer powerful performance with reduced computational costs and smaller memory footprints, have emerged as key players in promoting sustainability and addressing ethical concerns. This chapter explores the environmental benefits of using compact AI models, with a particular focus on their energy efficiency, as well as the ethical considerations that come with AI development and deployment.

---

1. The Environmental Impact of AI: Energy Consumption and Carbon Footprint

Background:

Large-scale AI models, especially in fields like natural language processing (NLP) and computer vision, have been known to consume vast amounts of computational resources. The energy consumption of training these models and running inference at scale has raised concerns regarding their environmental impact. Training large models can result in considerable carbon emissions, depending on the energy sources used by data centers and cloud computing services.

Key Insights:

- **Energy-Intensive Training**: Training large language models (LLMs) and other AI systems often requires powerful GPUs and TPUs, leading to significant electricity consumption. A study by researchers from the University of Massachusetts Amherst found that training large models can result in the emission of hundreds of tons of CO2, comparable to the lifetime emissions of an average car.
- **Operational Energy Demand**: Once trained, models require energy for inference, especially when deployed in applications that require real-time decision-making or are accessed by millions of users globally.

---

2. How Compact Models Contribute to Energy Efficiency

Background:

Compact AI models are designed to be lightweight, requiring less computational power for both training and inference. These models can significantly reduce the energy consumption associated with deploying AI systems.

Key Benefits:

- **Reduced Training Time and Energy**: Small models are generally quicker to train, needing fewer resources, lower memory, and less computational power. Techniques such as pruning, quantization, and distillation allow for reducing the model size while maintaining much of the performance of larger models.

  - **Pruning** removes unnecessary weights and connections in a model.
  - **Quantization** reduces the precision of the weights in the model, making the computation more efficient.
  - **Distillation** involves training a smaller "student" model to replicate the performance of a larger "teacher" model, which results in better energy efficiency.

- **Lower Operational Energy Costs**: Since compact models have fewer parameters, they can be deployed on less powerful hardware (such as edge devices and mobile phones), reducing the operational energy footprint.
  - **Edge AI**: Deploying compact models on edge devices, rather than relying on centralized cloud services, reduces the need for high-bandwidth data transfers and minimizes latency, contributing to energy savings.

Impact:

- **Global Carbon Reduction**: The widespread adoption of energy-efficient compact models can reduce the carbon footprint of AI technologies, contributing to global efforts to mitigate climate change.
- **Scalability**: As small models are easier to deploy on a wide range of devices, from smartphones to IoT devices, they facilitate the broad adoption of AI in a more sustainable manner.

---

3. Ethical Considerations: Accessibility and Fairness

Background:

While the environmental benefits of compact models are clear, there are also ethical considerations associated with their use. Compact models are not only more energy-efficient but also offer greater accessibility, especially in low-resource settings, which is crucial for promoting fairness in AI development.

Key Ethical Benefits:

- **Democratizing AI**: Compact models can be deployed on a wider variety of devices, including those in underprivileged and remote areas. This democratizes access to AI technologies, ensuring that more people, especially in developing countries, benefit from advancements in AI without requiring high-end computational infrastructure.
    - **Affordability**: Compact models are more cost-effective to train and deploy, making AI technologies accessible to a broader range of individuals and organizations.
    - **Localized Applications**: Compact models can be tailored to local languages, cultures, and contexts, improving fairness in AI application and reducing biases that may exist in large-scale, centralized models.
- **Data Privacy and Security**: Compact models, particularly those deployed on edge devices, can provide improved privacy by allowing data to be processed locally, rather than transmitted to centralized servers. This reduces the risks associated with data breaches and unauthorized access to sensitive personal data.
    - **Edge AI for Privacy**: Data such as health information, personal preferences, and financial details can be processed on local devices without compromising privacy, ensuring that individuals maintain control over their own data.

---

4. Ethical Challenges and Considerations

Background:

While compact models bring many benefits, there are

ethical challenges that need to be addressed to ensure their responsible deployment.

Key Challenges:

- **Bias and Fairness**: Despite their smaller size, compact models can still inherit biases from the data they are trained on. Since small models often rely on limited data, they may be more susceptible to overfitting or capturing biases that could affect marginalized or underrepresented groups.
  - **Solution**: Ensuring fairness in compact models requires careful attention to data diversity, implementing bias detection and correction algorithms, and validating models in a variety of real-world scenarios to ensure they function equitably for all users.
- **Job Displacement**: The automation capabilities enabled by compact models, especially in areas like customer service and manufacturing, could lead to job displacement, particularly for low-skilled workers. While AI offers productivity gains, it also necessitates a reevaluation of labor markets and the role of humans in an AI-driven economy.
  - **Solution**: Ethical considerations should include retraining programs, reskilling initiatives, and measures to ensure that AI technologies complement human workers rather than replacing them entirely.

---

5. Long-Term Sustainability: A Balanced Approach

Background:

The shift toward compact models is part of a broader effort to make AI more sustainable, ethical, and accessible. However, to ensure the long-term viability of AI technologies, it is important to balance innovation with responsibility.

Key Considerations for Sustainability:

- **Energy-Efficient Infrastructure**: In addition to compact models, companies must prioritize energy-efficient infrastructure in their data centers and cloud computing platforms. Renewable energy sources, such as solar and wind, should be integrated into AI infrastructure to reduce the carbon footprint of large-scale AI operations.
- **AI Governance**: Ethical AI deployment should include transparency in decision-making, accountability for AI systems' impact, and continuous monitoring of environmental and social effects.
- **Collaboration**: Collaboration between governments, research institutions, and the private sector is essential to create guidelines, standards, and policies that ensure AI technologies, including compact models, contribute positively to society.

Conclusion

Compact language models not only offer tangible environmental benefits by reducing energy consumption and operational costs, but they also present a more ethical path for AI development. These models promote accessibility, reduce data privacy concerns, and help ensure fairness in AI deployment, especially in low-resource and marginalized settings. However, the ethical challenges associated with bias, fairness, and job displacement must be carefully managed. By advancing energy-efficient and responsible AI practices, compact models are paving the way for a more sustainable, equitable, and accessible AI future.

ENVIRONMENTAL AND ETHICAL PERSPECTIVES: ADDRESSING BIAS IN SMALL LANGUAGE MODELS

As small language models become increasingly integral to various industries, their potential for promoting efficiency and accessibility is undeniable. However, with their growing presence in real-world applications, there are critical ethical considerations that must be addressed, particularly around the issue of **bias**. Bias in AI models is a well-documented concern, as it can perpetuate and amplify societal inequalities. While compact AI models offer environmental benefits through reduced computational resource usage, they also carry the risk of inheriting and amplifying biases present in training data.

This chapter explores the ethical implications of bias in small language models, the potential environmental impact of biased AI systems, and practical strategies to mitigate bias in their design and deployment.

---

1. Understanding Bias in Language Models

Background:

Bias in AI models refers to systematic and unfair discrimination in the outcomes generated by these systems. In the context of language models, bias can manifest in various ways, such as gender, racial, or socio-economic bias, often reflecting stereotypes present in the training data.

Types of Bias in Small Language Models:

- **Data Bias**: Language models learn from vast corpora of text data, and if the data contains historical biases or imbalances, the model will likely reproduce these biases. For instance, a model trained predominantly on text from Western sources may underrepresent non-Western languages and cultures.
- **Label Bias**: When training data is manually labeled, there is a risk that the labeling process itself introduces bias, whether from subjective human judgment or skewed sampling.
- **Algorithmic Bias**: Even with balanced data, the algorithms and model architectures themselves may introduce biases. This can occur due to poor model design, unintentional preferences in the training process, or the lack of diverse representation in the development team.

---

2. Environmental and Ethical Implications of Bias

Environmental Impact of Biased Models:

While compact models generally offer environmental benefits by reducing energy consumption, biased models can unintentionally lead to wasteful resource usage in several ways:

- **Increased Training Cycles**: Models with biases may require multiple rounds of retraining and fine-tuning to address their ethical shortcomings. This can negate the energy efficiency gains offered by small models.

- **Resource Wastage in Real-World Applications**: Biased decisions made by AI systems (e.g., in hiring or lending decisions) can lead to inefficiencies and wasted resources. For example, if a biased hiring model excludes qualified candidates based on gender or ethnicity, it could reduce workforce diversity and result in the underutilization of talent.

Ethical Concerns:

- **Amplification of Social Inequality**: Biased models can perpetuate and exacerbate existing social inequalities. For example, biased language models might discriminate against underrepresented groups in hiring, legal proceedings, or healthcare. This could result in marginalized populations being unfairly treated or overlooked.
- **Discrimination and Harm**: In sensitive applications, such as medical diagnostics or loan approvals, biased models could have harmful consequences, leading to poorer outcomes for affected individuals or communities.

---

3. Causes of Bias in Small Language Models

Background:

Small language models, while more energy-efficient and accessible, are still susceptible to bias due to several factors in the development and deployment process.

Key Causes of Bias:

- **Limited Training Data**: Small models often rely on smaller, more domain-specific datasets, which can increase the likelihood of overfitting to biased data.

The smaller the dataset, the more susceptible the model is to reflecting the biases inherent in the available text.

- **Insufficient Data Diversity**: Even with compact models, if the training data lacks diversity in terms of language, culture, gender, and geographical representation, the model will likely show biased behavior.
- **Simplified Algorithms**: While compact models benefit from reduced complexity, this simplification can sometimes cause unintended biases to be more pronounced or harder to detect. For instance, the model might rely heavily on features that encode socio-cultural stereotypes, such as the frequent co-occurrence of words like "doctor" with male pronouns in English texts.

---

4. Mitigating Bias in Small Language Models

Strategies for Bias Reduction:

Despite the challenges, there are effective strategies to address bias in small language models, ensuring they remain ethical and inclusive.

- **Data Curation and Augmentation**: Ensuring that training datasets are diverse and representative is critical. This includes using data from various cultural, linguistic, and socio-economic backgrounds to prevent the model from inheriting biased tendencies.
    - **Balanced Sampling**: By carefully selecting data from underrepresented groups or domains, developers can ensure the model is exposed to a broad spectrum of perspectives, minimizing the risk of biased predictions.
    - **Synthetic Data Generation**: For low-resource languages or specific domains, generating

synthetic data can help create more balanced datasets, which can be used to train models that are less likely to exhibit bias.

- **Bias Detection and Auditing**: Regular auditing of AI models to detect and mitigate biases is crucial. Automated tools and manual inspection of model predictions can help identify areas where the model may be making biased decisions.
  - **Fairness Testing**: Use fairness metrics such as demographic parity, equal opportunity, and disparate impact to evaluate model performance across different groups. This can guide developers in improving the model's ethical outcomes.
- **Explainable AI (XAI)**: Implementing explainable AI techniques helps users and developers understand how and why models make specific predictions, offering insights into whether and how bias may be influencing model behavior. This transparency is essential for accountability.
  - **Model Transparency**: Ensuring that model decisions are interpretable can help detect biases, improve accountability, and facilitate debugging.
  - **Human-in-the-Loop**: In critical applications, having a human check and validate AI-driven decisions can prevent the reinforcement of biased outcomes.
- **Fairness-Focused Model Training**: Special algorithms and techniques, such as **adversarial debiasing**, can be applied during the training phase to ensure that models minimize bias and avoid learning from discriminatory patterns in the data.
  - **Adversarial Debiasing**: This technique involves introducing an adversarial network that penalizes the model whenever it generates biased outcomes, encouraging

the model to learn more balanced representations.

---

5. Ethical Responsibility of Developers and Organizations

Background:

The development and deployment of small language models carry ethical responsibility. Developers, organizations, and researchers must remain vigilant in addressing bias and ensuring that their AI systems are aligned with societal values of fairness, transparency, and accountability.

Ethical Responsibilities:

- **Inclusive Development Teams**: Ensuring diversity within development teams is essential. Teams composed of individuals with varied backgrounds can help recognize biases and prevent them from being inadvertently embedded in the model.
- **Stakeholder Engagement**: Involving relevant stakeholders, such as community representatives, ethicists, and domain experts, in the model development process can ensure that the AI system aligns with broader social norms and ethical standards.
- **Accountability and Governance**: Organizations must adopt clear governance frameworks to oversee AI development. This includes setting up independent review boards, establishing ethical guidelines, and ensuring ongoing monitoring of AI deployment.

---

6. Case Studies and Real-World Examples

Real-World Examples of Bias Mitigation:

Several organizations and research groups are actively working on addressing bias in small language models.

Examples include:

- **Google's Inclusive AI Efforts**: Google's AI teams have prioritized fairness and inclusivity by implementing fairness audits and using diverse datasets in the training of their models, addressing concerns around biased search results and language processing.
- **Microsoft's AI Ethics Toolkit**: Microsoft's toolkit includes guidelines for identifying and mitigating bias in AI models. The company has also launched initiatives to increase the diversity of their AI models to better represent global cultures and languages.

Conclusion

Addressing bias in small language models is not just a technical challenge; it is a core ethical responsibility for AI developers and organizations. While these models offer energy efficiency and scalability, they must be developed and deployed with a strong emphasis on fairness, inclusivity, and transparency. By implementing strategies for bias detection, data diversification, and fairness-focused training, we can ensure that small models contribute to a more just, equitable, and environmentally responsible future for AI. Through ongoing collaboration and commitment to ethical principles, AI systems, regardless of their size, can be harnessed to benefit all segments of society.

ENVIRONMENTAL AND ETHICAL PERSPECTIVES: ENSURING DATA PRIVACY AND SECURITY

As small language models (SLMs) continue to gain traction in diverse applications—from healthcare to customer service—ensuring data privacy and security has become a critical concern. While these models offer a host of benefits, including energy efficiency and reduced computational costs, they must be handled with care when it comes to managing sensitive data. Small language models are often deployed in environments where they interact with personal, financial, and health-related data, making data privacy and security not only a legal requirement but also a fundamental ethical responsibility.

This chapter explores the challenges and ethical considerations involved in securing data in small language models, outlining strategies and techniques for ensuring privacy, compliance with regulations, and maintaining the trust of end-users.

---

1. The Need for Data Privacy in Small Language Models

Background:

Data privacy refers to the protection of personal information from unauthorized access, use, or disclosure. In the context of AI and machine learning, data privacy becomes especially critical because these systems often rely on vast amounts of personal data to function effectively.

For small language models, which are frequently used in edge computing or in low-resource environments, the stakes of data privacy are high. If not properly handled, these models can inadvertently expose or misuse personal information, leading to breaches of confidentiality and undermining user trust.

Key Considerations for Data Privacy:

- **Data Sensitivity**: SLMs may process sensitive data such as medical records, financial transactions, or personal identifiers. Unauthorized access to such data can lead to significant privacy violations.
- **Data Minimization**: One of the main principles in data privacy is that only the minimum necessary data should be collected and used. SLMs should be designed to avoid storing or processing unnecessary sensitive information unless absolutely required.
- **User Consent**: Ethical deployment of AI models requires that users provide informed consent before their data is processed. This is particularly important in sectors such as healthcare, where patient information is highly sensitive.

---

2. Security Risks in Small Language Models

Background:

While small language models are often praised for their computational efficiency, they may also present unique security challenges. Smaller models may rely on edge devices, where the security infrastructure can be less robust compared to centralized servers. Additionally, the more compact nature of these models may reduce the amount of security controls that can be implemented.

Key Security Risks:

- **Data Leakage**: In some cases, language models may inadvertently leak sensitive information through the text they generate. This could happen if the model was trained on proprietary or sensitive data without proper anonymization or safeguards.
- **Model Inversion Attacks**: Small language models may be more vulnerable to attacks that reverse-engineer the model to extract sensitive training data. In a model inversion attack, an adversary could query the model to obtain details about the training data, potentially exposing private information.
- **Adversarial Attacks**: As with other AI models, SLMs are also vulnerable to adversarial attacks, where malicious actors manipulate input data to trick the model into generating incorrect or harmful outputs. These attacks could be used to compromise the security of applications, particularly in areas such as finance or healthcare.

---

3. Legal and Regulatory Frameworks

Background:

To address data privacy and security concerns, numerous legal and regulatory frameworks have been established globally. These laws provide the foundation for organizations to build secure and privacy-compliant systems, ensuring that both personal data and AI models are protected.

Key Regulations:

- **General Data Protection Regulation (GDPR)**: This

European regulation provides stringent guidelines for the processing and storage of personal data. It mandates that data controllers ensure that AI systems, including language models, do not violate user privacy rights, and that users have the right to access, correct, and delete their personal data.

- **Health Insurance Portability and Accountability Act (HIPAA)**: In the U.S., HIPAA sets standards for the privacy and security of health information. SLMs used in healthcare applications must comply with these standards to protect patient data.
- **California Consumer Privacy Act (CCPA)**: A key privacy law in California, the CCPA mandates that businesses give consumers the right to access and delete their personal data, offering them greater control over how their information is used.

Compliance Challenges:

- **Data Sovereignty**: Laws such as the GDPR often require that data remain within specific geographic boundaries, which can create challenges when small language models are deployed on edge devices or in distributed networks.
- **Auditability and Transparency**: Ensuring that small models are auditable and transparent is a key part of regulatory compliance. This includes providing clear records of data usage and model decisions, which is often difficult in compact AI systems due to their smaller scale and simplified architecture.

---

4. Strategies for Ensuring Data Privacy in Small Language Models

Data Encryption:

- **End-to-End Encryption**: One of the most effective

methods for protecting sensitive data is to use end-to-end encryption. This ensures that data is encrypted both when stored and when transmitted, preventing unauthorized access at any stage of the process.

- **Differential Privacy**: Differential privacy is a technique that adds noise to data or model predictions to prevent individuals' information from being identifiable. It's particularly useful when working with small language models that may process sensitive user data. By adding random noise to the data, it becomes difficult for any observer to extract information about specific individuals.

Federated Learning:

- **Federated Learning** allows small language models to be trained on distributed devices (e.g., mobile phones or IoT devices) without the need to centralize data. This approach minimizes the risk of exposing sensitive data because the data never leaves the device; only model updates are shared.
    - **Benefits**: Federated learning allows privacy to be maintained while still enabling models to be trained on diverse data. Additionally, since the data remains local, the risk of a data breach is reduced.

Data Anonymization and De-identification:

- **Anonymization**: Removing personally identifiable information (PII) from training datasets helps mitigate the risk of privacy violations. Anonymized data cannot be traced back to individual users, ensuring that sensitive details remain protected.

- **De-identification**: Similar to anonymization, de-identification removes identifying details from data but allows for some level of re-identification under certain controlled circumstances. This balance helps maintain privacy while enabling data to be used for useful analysis.

---

5. Security Measures for Protecting Small Language Models

Model Encryption and Access Control:

- **Model Encryption**: Encrypting the model weights and the training process itself can prevent adversarial actors from stealing or tampering with the model.
- **Access Control**: Implementing strict access control mechanisms ensures that only authorized parties can interact with the model. This is especially critical when small language models are deployed on edge devices with limited security infrastructure.

Robust Authentication and Authorization:

- **Multi-Factor Authentication (MFA)**: Requiring multiple forms of authentication, such as passwords and biometrics, can help secure access to the model and the data it processes.
- **Role-Based Access Control (RBAC)**: This approach ensures that different users have different levels of access to the model, based on their role within the organization.

Adversarial Robustness:

- **Adversarial Training**: Small language models can be exposed to adversarial examples during training to enhance their robustness against attacks. By training the model to identify and defend against malicious inputs, developers can reduce the likelihood of adversarial vulnerabilities.

---

6. Best Practices for Ethical Data Privacy and Security

Privacy by Design:

Incorporating privacy considerations into the design and development of small language models from the outset ensures that privacy is built into the system rather than tacked on afterward. This approach includes:

- **Data Minimization**: Only collect and use the data that is necessary for the model's function.
- **Security Audits**: Regular security audits can identify vulnerabilities and ensure compliance with privacy regulations.

Transparency and User Empowerment:

- **Informed Consent**: Users must be informed about how their data will be used and have the option to consent to it. Clear, accessible privacy policies and consent forms are essential.
- **User Control**: Allowing users to manage their data, including access to their personal information and the ability to delete it, is crucial for maintaining trust.

Conclusion

Ensuring data privacy and security in small language models is both a technical challenge and an ethical responsibility. As these models continue to shape the future of AI applications, developers, organizations, and policymakers must prioritize privacy protection and adopt strategies to secure sensitive data. By implementing robust encryption, federated learning, data anonymization, and security protocols, small language models can be deployed in a secure, privacy-conscious manner. This will not only foster trust among users but also ensure that small models can be safely and ethically used in various industries, from healthcare to finance, while complying with global privacy regulations.

FUTURE DIRECTIONS IN COMPACT AI: ADVANCEMENTS IN MODEL COMPRESSION TECHNIQUES

As the demand for more efficient artificial intelligence (AI) continues to grow, the need for compact AI models that are both lightweight and powerful has become increasingly apparent. Compact models, particularly small language models (SLMs), are essential for deployment in resource-constrained environments, such as mobile devices, edge computing, and IoT ecosystems. However, to maintain their high performance while reducing their size, significant advances in model compression techniques are required. In this chapter, we will explore the future directions in compact AI, with a specific focus on the latest advancements in model compression techniques, and how these developments are shaping the next generation of AI systems.

---

1. The Importance of Model Compression in Compact AI

Background:

Model compression is the process of reducing the size of a machine learning model while maintaining or improving its performance. The need for model compression arises from the growing requirement to deploy AI models in environments with limited computational resources, such as mobile phones, edge devices, and other low-power systems.

For small language models (SLMs) and other compact AI systems, model compression plays a crucial role in ensuring that they can function efficiently without sacrificing accuracy. By compressing models, it becomes feasible to deploy AI solutions in real-time applications that require low latency and low energy consumption.

Key Benefits of Model Compression:

- **Reduced Memory and Storage Requirements**: Smaller models require less memory and storage space, making them suitable for environments with limited resources.
- **Faster Inference**: Compressed models tend to require less computation, leading to faster processing times and reduced latency.
- **Lower Power Consumption**: With smaller models, energy usage is reduced, making it ideal for battery-operated devices.

---

2. Emerging Techniques in Model Compression

While several established techniques for model compression —such as pruning, quantization, and distillation—have been used effectively, new and improved methods are emerging. Below are some of the most promising advancements in the field.

a. Structured Pruning and Sparsity

- **Structured Pruning** involves removing entire neurons, filters, or layers from the model, as opposed to unstructured pruning, which removes individual weights. The goal is to preserve the model's structure while reducing its size.

- **Advancement**: Recent advances in structured pruning focus on creating more efficient pruning strategies that better maintain the performance of the model even after significant reduction. Techniques like **block-wise pruning** allow for large-scale compression while maintaining overall accuracy.
- **Impact**: This approach ensures that models are not just smaller, but also maintain a high level of interpretability and efficiency.

b. Knowledge Distillation

- **Knowledge Distillation** is the process of transferring knowledge from a large, pre-trained model (teacher) to a smaller model (student). The student model is trained to mimic the output of the teacher model, enabling it to retain high performance with fewer parameters.
    - **Advancement**: New developments in distillation techniques are focusing on multi-teacher distillation, where the student model is trained with knowledge from multiple teacher models, allowing for more diverse learning and better generalization.
    - **Impact**: These advancements in distillation are leading to even smaller models that perform almost as well as their larger counterparts, opening up new possibilities for deploying AI at the edge.

c. Quantization

- **Quantization** refers to reducing the precision of the model weights, converting them from floating-point numbers to lower bit-width representations, such as 8-bit integers. This reduces the memory footprint and speeds up inference.

- **Advancement**: Techniques like **mixed-precision quantization** are being explored, where certain parts of the model are quantized more aggressively than others, based on their importance for performance. This method allows for further reductions in size without compromising accuracy.
- **Impact**: As hardware accelerators become more powerful, quantization techniques can lead to highly efficient models that perform real-time processing on resource-constrained devices.

d. Neural Architecture Search (NAS)

- **Neural Architecture Search** involves using algorithms to search for the most efficient model architecture for a given task. By automating the design of smaller, efficient models, NAS can discover novel architectures that are more compact while still performing well.
  - **Advancement**: New NAS techniques are focusing on searching for architectures that are not only small but also optimized for specific hardware, such as mobile processors or GPUs. **One-shot NAS** allows for faster and more scalable searches by evaluating multiple architectures simultaneously.
  - **Impact**: NAS techniques could revolutionize the process of creating compact AI models, making it easier to build optimized, application-specific models that are small and fast.

e. Weight Sharing and Low-Rank Factorization

- **Weight Sharing** involves forcing different weights in the neural network to share the same parameters, which can drastically reduce the model size.
- **Low-Rank Factorization** decomposes the weight

matrices in neural networks into lower-rank matrices, reducing the number of parameters.

- **Advancement**: Both techniques are being combined with other compression methods, such as pruning and distillation, to achieve even greater compression without sacrificing performance.
- **Impact**: These methods allow for significant compression, which is especially important for models deployed in environments where computational resources are extremely limited.

---

3. The Role of Hardware in Supporting Compact AI Models

As model compression techniques advance, the role of specialized hardware in supporting these models is becoming more significant. Emerging hardware accelerators, such as **TPUs (Tensor Processing Units)**, **ASICs (Application-Specific Integrated Circuits)**, and **FPGAs (Field-Programmable Gate Arrays)**, are designed to work seamlessly with compressed models, allowing for faster execution of small models without the need for heavy computational resources.

- **AI Accelerators**: The development of AI chips optimized for running compact models is enabling the next wave of AI applications in resource-constrained environments. These chips are designed to handle the low-precision calculations required by quantized models and can accelerate inference in real-time.
- **Edge Devices**: Compact AI models will thrive in edge computing environments, where they can run locally on devices like smartphones, wearables, and IoT sensors without needing constant communication with cloud servers. The combination of hardware advancements and compressed models will enable AI to become ubiquitous in everyday life.

4. Open Challenges and Future Research Directions

Despite the exciting advancements in model compression, several challenges remain:

a. Performance vs. Compression Trade-off

One of the primary challenges in model compression is maintaining high performance while reducing the model size. While techniques like pruning and quantization can significantly reduce model size, they may lead to accuracy degradation. Finding the right balance between model compression and performance is an ongoing area of research.

b. Generalization Across Domains

Many compression techniques work well in specific domains or tasks, but their effectiveness can vary when applied to new domains or problem sets. Researchers are working to develop universal compression techniques that can generalize across a wide range of applications.

c. Real-Time Adaptation

As small language models become more widely deployed in real-time applications, the need for models to adapt quickly to new data and changing conditions will become more pressing. Compression techniques must evolve to support continuous learning without requiring large-scale retraining or updates.

5. Conclusion

The future of compact AI models lies in continued advancements in model compression techniques. By making small language models more efficient and lightweight, these techniques open up new possibilities for deploying AI across a wide range of industries, from healthcare to autonomous vehicles. As we move toward a future where AI is seamlessly integrated into our everyday devices, model compression will be a key enabler in delivering powerful, efficient, and ethical AI solutions that are accessible to everyone.

Through ongoing innovation in techniques like pruning, quantization, distillation, and NAS, compact AI will continue to evolve, making it more efficient, flexible, and applicable in diverse environments. As these models become even more refined, their potential to solve real-world problems will be limitless, offering AI-driven solutions that are both impactful and sustainable.

FUTURE DIRECTIONS IN COMPACT AI: INTEGRATING SMALL MODELS WITH LARGER AI ECOSYSTEMS

As artificial intelligence (AI) continues to evolve, the need for compact models that can operate in resource-constrained environments has become increasingly important. Small models, particularly small language models (SLMs), are being deployed in a variety of use cases—from mobile devices and IoT to real-time data processing and edge computing. However, as AI ecosystems grow in complexity, there is a growing need for these small models to integrate seamlessly with larger, more powerful models and systems. This chapter explores the future directions in integrating small AI models with larger AI ecosystems, ensuring that the potential of both small and large models is harnessed to deliver efficient, scalable, and effective AI solutions.

---

1. The Role of Small Models in Large AI Ecosystems

Small models play an important role in AI ecosystems,

particularly in environments where resource efficiency is paramount. While large models often provide cutting-edge performance and versatility, they require significant computational resources, storage, and energy consumption. In contrast, small models offer the following advantages:

- **Efficiency**: They can run in low-resource environments such as mobile devices, IoT systems, and edge devices.
- **Real-Time Processing**: Small models are often capable of performing tasks with low latency, making them ideal for applications that require real-time decision-making.
- **Scalability**: By using small models, AI can be deployed at scale, even in remote or resource-constrained locations.

However, small models must be able to collaborate and integrate effectively with larger models to achieve the full potential of the AI ecosystem. The challenge lies in ensuring that these models can work together in harmony, leveraging the strengths of both small and large models.

---

2. Hybrid Architectures: Combining Small and Large Models

One of the most promising approaches to integrating small models with larger AI ecosystems is the use of **hybrid architectures**. A hybrid system typically involves combining the capabilities of both small and large models, allowing them to complement each other.

a. Cascading Models

In a cascading architecture, small models handle simpler tasks and pre-processing, while larger models are used for more complex tasks. This tiered approach allows the system to make efficient use of resources by offloading computationally intensive tasks to the larger model only when necessary.

- **Example**: In a natural language processing (NLP) system, a small model could perform initial tasks like keyword extraction or sentiment classification. If the input is more complex, the system could then pass the data to a larger model for more in-depth analysis, such as contextual language understanding or translation.

b. Model Offloading

Another approach is model offloading, where small models are deployed on edge devices, and more complex models are run on centralized cloud servers or data centers. This setup allows small models to operate independently for certain tasks, while offloading intensive computations to larger models when needed.

- **Example**: In an autonomous vehicle system, small models on the vehicle could handle immediate tasks like obstacle detection using sensors, while larger models in the cloud handle more complex tasks, such as decision-making and route planning.

c. Parallel Processing

In this approach, both small and large models are run in parallel, with tasks divided between them based on their complexity. Small models can handle routine or well-defined tasks, while larger models focus on more intricate or ambiguous tasks. This method can improve processing speed and overall system efficiency.

- **Example**: In healthcare diagnostics, small models could be used for preliminary screenings or flagging potential issues, while larger models perform more complex analysis based on a broader range of data.

---

3. Model Fusion: Combining the Strengths of Small and Large Models

Model fusion refers to the process of combining the output of small and large models to create a unified result. Instead of having separate models perform tasks independently, the outputs of different models can be integrated to leverage the strengths of both.

a. Ensemble Learning

Ensemble learning involves combining predictions from multiple models, including both small and large models, to improve accuracy and robustness. By using a diverse set of models, the system can reduce the likelihood of errors and make more reliable predictions.

- **Example**: In predictive analytics, a system could combine the outputs of small models (which might excel at handling high-frequency data) with larger models (which are better at identifying complex patterns) to generate more accurate forecasts.

b. Feature Fusion

In feature fusion, small and large models are trained to focus on different aspects of the input data. The features extracted by small models can be combined with those extracted by larger models to enhance the system's ability to learn complex patterns and make more nuanced predictions.

- **Example**: In a recommendation system, small models might focus on processing basic user preferences (e.g., recent interactions or ratings), while large models analyze deeper user behavior patterns (e.g., long-term preferences or context-aware recommendations). The features from both models can then be fused to deliver more personalized recommendations.

---

4. Multi-Task Learning with Small and Large Models

Multi-task learning is a powerful technique where a single model or set of models is trained to perform multiple tasks simultaneously. This approach can be extended to integrate small and large models in a way that allows them to work on different tasks within the same ecosystem.

a. Task Allocation Between Small and Large Models

In a multi-task learning framework, small models can be allocated tasks that are less computationally expensive, while large models focus on tasks that require deep learning or more sophisticated analysis. By carefully dividing tasks, the system can operate efficiently without overloading the resources.

- **Example**: In a voice assistant, small models can handle basic commands (e.g., play music, set reminders), while larger models can process more complex requests, such as understanding user intent or conducting multi-step reasoning.

b. Shared Representations

In multi-task learning, small and large models can share common representations or intermediate layers, allowing them to learn from each other's strengths. The small model can focus on learning specific representations for certain tasks, while the large model can refine these representations to improve overall performance.

- **Example**: In an image recognition system, a small model might detect basic objects (e.g., shapes, colors), while a larger model could be used to identify more complex objects (e.g., animals, vehicles). The representations learned by the small model could be shared with the larger model for better performance.

---

5. Federated Learning: Distributed AI with Small and Large Models

Federated learning enables distributed training of AI models across multiple devices while keeping data local. In this scenario, small models can be deployed on edge devices, and the knowledge they learn can be aggregated into a central model, which could be large and powerful.

a. Collaborative Learning

In federated learning, small models can learn from data on individual devices, while large models in the cloud aggregate the knowledge and improve over time. The small models can be fine-tuned locally, while the large models can combine insights from multiple small models to enhance performance.

- **Example**: In healthcare, small models on wearable devices can monitor patient vitals and collect data, while large models in a centralized cloud server analyze the aggregated data from multiple devices to detect patterns and provide recommendations.

b. Privacy-Preserving AI

Federated learning allows for privacy-preserving AI, where the data never leaves the edge devices, and only model updates are shared with the central server. This ensures that small models can be used to collect and process sensitive data without compromising privacy, while larger models benefit from the distributed knowledge.

- **Example**: In financial services, small models on mobile devices can process transaction data to detect fraud, while larger models in a centralized server analyze broader patterns and correlations across users.

---

6. The Future of Integrating Small Models with Large AI Ecosystems

The integration of small models with larger AI ecosystems will continue to be a key area of innovation. As AI becomes more pervasive in everyday life, it will require intelligent systems that can combine the efficiency of small models with the power and versatility of large models. The following trends will shape the future of these integrations:

- **Increased Edge Intelligence**: More AI tasks will be offloaded to the edge, allowing for faster, more localized decision-making with the collaboration of small and large models.
- **Cross-Model Collaboration**: Hybrid and multi-task systems will become more common, with small and large models working in tandem to deliver better results.
- **Seamless Cloud-Edge Integration**: The integration between cloud-based large models and edge-deployed small models will become more streamlined, allowing for a dynamic exchange of information and processing capabilities.

Ultimately, the ability to integrate small models with larger AI ecosystems will enable more efficient, scalable, and real-time AI applications across a wide variety of industries—from healthcare to smart cities and beyond.

Conclusion

The integration of small models with larger AI ecosystems is an exciting frontier in the development of compact AI solutions. By combining the strengths of both small and large models, organizations can create more efficient, scalable, and adaptable AI systems. As model compression, hybrid architectures, and federated learning continue to evolve, the future of AI will be shaped by these integrated, multi-dimensional systems that provide smarter, faster, and more energy-efficient solutions across industries.

FUTURE DIRECTIONS IN COMPACT AI: THE ROLE OF SMALL AI IN DEMOCRATIZING TECHNOLOGY

As artificial intelligence (AI) continues to advance, the focus is increasingly shifting toward making AI more accessible, scalable, and efficient. One of the most significant trends in this direction is the rise of **compact AI**, particularly small models, which have the potential to **democratize technology** across the globe. Small AI models, especially small language models (SLMs), are unlocking new opportunities to integrate AI into a wide array of industries, devices, and applications, especially in regions and sectors with limited access to powerful computing infrastructure. This chapter explores how small AI is poised to democratize technology, making AI-driven solutions more available and impactful to individuals, businesses, and societies worldwide.

---

1. The Promise of Small AI in Bridging the Digital Divide

The **digital divide** refers to the disparity in access to technology and information between different regions, socio-economic groups, and countries. Traditionally, powerful AI models have required significant computational resources

—often only available to large corporations or countries with advanced technological infrastructures. However, small AI models have the potential to bridge this gap by making advanced AI tools accessible in resource-constrained environments.

a. Accessibility in Low-Resource Environments

Small AI models are designed to be computationally efficient, requiring less memory, processing power, and energy consumption. This makes them suitable for deployment in **low-resource environments**, such as rural areas, developing economies, and remote locations.

- **Example**: In regions with limited access to cloud-based services or high-performance computing, small models can be deployed on local devices like smartphones or low-cost hardware, allowing users to access AI tools without needing a fast internet connection or expensive infrastructure.

b. Empowering Local Communities

With the accessibility of small AI, local communities can directly benefit from AI technology without relying on centralized systems. Small AI can power applications such as healthcare diagnostics, agriculture monitoring, and education tools, giving individuals the ability to leverage AI for local problem-solving.

- **Example**: Small models can be integrated into mobile health applications that allow individuals in underserved regions to diagnose common ailments and receive real-time medical advice, even in areas with limited access to healthcare professionals.

---

2. Small AI Models for Accessibility in Education and Learning

Education is another area where compact AI models can play

a transformative role in democratizing technology. Access to quality education and learning tools is often limited by geographic, economic, or social factors. Small AI can help bridge this gap by providing personalized and scalable learning experiences.

a. Personalized Learning on Mobile Devices

Small AI models can be embedded into **mobile learning platforms**, providing personalized recommendations and feedback for learners. These models can adapt to individual learning styles and progress, helping students in remote or underserved areas access educational content tailored to their needs.

- **Example**: AI-powered educational apps on smartphones can assess students' understanding of subjects like mathematics or languages and provide customized exercises or explanations, enabling learning on the go without relying on expensive hardware or online connectivity.

b. Support for Special Needs Education

Small AI models can also assist in **special needs education**, offering personalized learning tools for children with disabilities. Compact AI solutions can be used for speech recognition, text-to-speech, and other adaptive technologies that support students with physical or cognitive challenges.

- **Example**: AI-driven speech recognition tools can assist children with speech impairments by providing real-time feedback, helping them communicate more effectively without the need for specialized, expensive hardware.

---

3. Small AI Enabling Affordable Healthcare in Underserved Regions

One of the most significant ways that small AI

is democratizing technology is by enabling **affordable healthcare** in regions where access to medical professionals, infrastructure, and resources is limited. Compact AI models can be deployed to assist in diagnostics, patient monitoring, and health education in a way that is both cost-effective and scalable.

a. Remote Diagnostics and Telemedicine

Small AI models can be integrated into **mobile health platforms** that provide diagnostics, consultations, and medical advice remotely. By analyzing symptoms or medical data captured via smartphones or basic devices, these models can offer insights that would typically require a healthcare professional, making basic health services more accessible.

- **Example**: In rural areas, small AI models can be used in diagnostic apps that analyze user inputs (e.g., symptoms, medical history) and provide preliminary diagnoses or recommendations, reducing the need for patients to travel long distances to visit a doctor.

b. Affordable Medical Devices

Compact AI can be embedded into **wearable devices** or low-cost medical instruments, offering monitoring services for conditions like hypertension, diabetes, or asthma. These AI-powered devices can alert individuals to potential health issues, encouraging early intervention and improving health outcomes.

- **Example**: Small AI models in wearable devices can monitor heart rate or blood sugar levels, providing real-time feedback and alerting users to any abnormal readings, which is particularly beneficial in areas with limited access to healthcare professionals.

---

4. Small AI in Agriculture: Empowering Small-Scale Farmers

Agriculture is one of the sectors that can benefit significantly from small AI models, especially in **developing countries** where small-scale farmers often lack access to advanced technology or modern agricultural practices. Compact AI can assist in optimizing farming techniques, improving crop yields, and reducing resource waste.

a. Precision Agriculture on Low-Cost Devices

Small AI models can be integrated into affordable **smart farming tools**, such as sensors or mobile apps, that help farmers monitor soil conditions, weather patterns, crop health, and pest activity. These tools provide real-time data and actionable insights, improving decision-making without requiring expensive infrastructure.

- **Example**: Small AI models embedded in low-cost soil sensors can analyze moisture levels and nutrient content, giving farmers timely advice on irrigation and fertilization to optimize crop growth.

b. Pest and Disease Detection

Compact AI models can analyze images from **low-cost cameras** or drones to detect pests, diseases, or deficiencies in crops. By providing early warnings, these models can help farmers take preventive action, reducing the reliance on pesticides and minimizing crop loss.

- **Example**: Small AI-powered drones or cameras can scan fields for signs of pest infestations, disease, or nutrient deficiencies, allowing farmers to address issues before they become widespread, ultimately improving yields and sustainability.

---

5. Empowering Small Businesses with Affordable AI Solutions

Small and medium-sized enterprises (SMEs) often face barriers when it comes to adopting AI due to high costs and a lack of technical expertise. Compact AI models are helping to remove these barriers, making AI technology more accessible and affordable for smaller businesses.

a. AI-Powered Customer Service for SMEs

Small businesses can integrate compact AI models into **customer service** platforms to automate responses to customer queries, manage bookings, and personalize communication, all without the need for expensive AI systems or large teams of customer service representatives.

- **Example**: A small retail business could use a small language model to handle basic customer queries about product availability, shipping, and returns, freeing up human agents for more complex interactions.

b. AI for Marketing and Sales

Small AI models can also be applied to **marketing automation**, helping small businesses analyze customer data, optimize marketing campaigns, and personalize offers. These AI-driven solutions can operate on inexpensive hardware and can be easily integrated with existing systems.

- **Example**: Compact AI models can power recommendation engines that suggest products to customers based on their browsing history, increasing sales for small e-commerce platforms.

---

6. The Role of Small AI in Promoting Global Sustainability

Compact AI models are also contributing to the **sustainable development goals (SDGs)** by providing solutions that promote environmental conservation, resource efficiency, and climate resilience, especially in regions where resources are scarce.

a. Energy-Efficient Solutions

Small AI models require significantly less energy than their larger counterparts, making them ideal for **energy-efficient applications**. By optimizing energy use in smart homes, manufacturing processes, and transportation systems, small AI can help reduce carbon footprints in industries and households.

- **Example**: In smart homes, small AI models can optimize heating, cooling, and lighting systems to minimize energy consumption, making it possible for households in energy-poor regions to access affordable energy solutions.

b. Environmental Monitoring

Small AI models can be deployed on low-cost sensors to monitor environmental factors like air quality, water pollution, and waste management, helping local communities track and mitigate environmental damage.

- **Example**: Small AI models on portable environmental sensors can monitor pollution levels in cities or remote areas, providing real-time data that can be used to take action and protect public health.

Conclusion: Small AI and the Future of Democratizing Technology

Small AI models are a catalyst for **democratizing technology**, breaking down the barriers to accessing powerful AI tools and making them available to a broader range of users, industries, and communities. As these models continue to evolve, they will empower individuals and organizations worldwide to unlock the potential of AI, improving quality of life, enhancing business efficiency, and driving sustainability in resource-constrained environments. The future of small AI is not just about reducing the size and complexity of models; it's about creating a more **inclusive and accessible future** where AI serves everyone, no matter where they live or how much they can invest in technology.

CASE STUDIES AND SUCCESS STORIES: COMPACT AI TRANSFORMING STARTUPS

Compact AI, particularly small language models and other efficient AI tools, are revolutionizing the way startups operate. Startups often face resource constraints, including limited budgets, small teams, and a need for rapid scalability. Small AI models, with their efficiency and low computational requirements, allow startups to leverage the power of artificial intelligence without requiring large-scale infrastructure. This chapter explores several **case studies and success stories** that showcase how startups are using compact AI to achieve remarkable outcomes in various industries.

---

1. Case Study: AI-Powered Customer Support for a SaaS Startup

Company: ZenoSupport, a Software-as-a-Service (SaaS) startup that provides cloud-based customer service solutions for small businesses.

Challenge:

ZenoSupport, a rapidly growing SaaS company, needed to

scale its customer support operations to meet the growing demand for its service. With limited resources, the startup faced challenges in hiring enough support staff to handle the increasing volume of customer inquiries while maintaining quality and response times.

Solution:

ZenoSupport implemented a **compact AI-driven chatbot** powered by a small language model designed for text-based customer service. The chatbot, deployed on their website and within the app, was trained to answer common questions about the platform, handle account-related issues, and direct users to relevant help articles.

- **Pruning and Distillation Techniques** were used to create a smaller, efficient version of the language model that could run on servers with limited processing power, significantly reducing operational costs.
- **Integration with CRM systems** allowed the chatbot to not only respond to queries but also log conversations and escalate complex issues to human agents.

Outcome:

The implementation of the small AI chatbot allowed ZenoSupport to **reduce response time** by 60%, handle 80% of customer inquiries without human intervention, and scale customer support without additional hires. The chatbot's efficiency, powered by compact AI, made it a cost-effective solution that enhanced the startup's scalability and customer satisfaction.

---

2. Case Study: AI-Powered Content Personalization for an E-Commerce Startup

Company: ShopSage, an e-commerce platform specializing in personalized home goods.

Challenge:

ShopSage was struggling to compete in a crowded e-commerce market where larger competitors offered highly personalized shopping experiences. The startup's challenge was to enhance product recommendations for users based on their browsing behavior, purchase history, and preferences, but it lacked the resources to implement complex AI models.

Solution:

ShopSage adopted **compact AI models** for product recommendation and personalization. Using techniques like **quantization** and **distillation**, the startup created a lightweight model that could generate product suggestions in real-time with minimal computational power. The model was deployed on the company's website and mobile app, analyzing customer behavior and recommending relevant products.

- **Pruning** techniques helped reduce the size of the recommendation model while retaining its effectiveness in making accurate predictions.
- The compact model was optimized for mobile and low-cost servers, ensuring that the platform could serve personalized recommendations to users without needing high-end cloud computing resources.

Outcome:

By implementing compact AI for product recommendations, ShopSage was able to **increase conversion rates** by 25%, significantly improving the shopping experience for customers. The compact nature of the AI model allowed the startup to offer a highly personalized service, which helped differentiate it in the competitive e-commerce market without requiring expensive infrastructure.

---

3. Case Study: Compact AI for Financial Fraud Detection in a FinTech Startup

Company: FinSecure, a financial technology startup focused on providing anti-fraud solutions for online transactions.

Challenge:

FinSecure's mission was to detect and prevent fraudulent transactions in real-time for its users. However, the startup's limited resources made it difficult to deploy traditional machine learning models that required large amounts of data processing and storage. FinSecure needed an efficient, cost-effective solution to monitor transactions across multiple channels in real time.

Solution:

FinSecure integrated a **compact AI model** for transaction monitoring and fraud detection. The model was trained on historical transaction data to identify patterns indicative of fraud, such as unusual spending behaviors or anomalies in user profiles.

- **Model compression techniques** like **quantization** and **distillation** were used to reduce the model size and enhance its speed without sacrificing accuracy. The compact AI was designed to run on low-cost cloud infrastructure, allowing FinSecure to process large volumes of transactions efficiently.
- The system integrated seamlessly with existing payment processing tools, providing real-time alerts for suspicious activity.

Outcome:

The deployment of the compact AI model resulted in a **50% reduction in false positives** while improving the accuracy of fraud detection. FinSecure was able to provide real-time fraud prevention for small to medium-sized businesses, offering a highly competitive service at a fraction of the cost of larger, traditional fraud detection systems.

---

4. Case Study: Compact AI in Predictive Maintenance for a Manufacturing Startup

Company: AutoMend, a manufacturing startup specializing in smart factory solutions and predictive maintenance for industrial machinery.

Challenge:

AutoMend wanted to introduce **predictive maintenance** to help small and medium-sized manufacturing businesses optimize their equipment performance and reduce downtime. However, the startup faced the challenge of integrating AI-driven predictive maintenance systems into factories that used low-cost or legacy machinery with limited connectivity and computing power.

Solution:

AutoMend developed a **compact AI model** to predict equipment failures by analyzing sensor data, temperature, vibration, and other performance indicators. The model was designed to run on **edge devices** with limited computing power, meaning it could be deployed directly on the factory floor without the need for expensive infrastructure or cloud connectivity.

- Techniques like **model pruning** were used to reduce the model's complexity while ensuring it could still provide accurate predictions based on real-time sensor data.
- The compact AI system provided predictive alerts on machinery malfunctions, which allowed manufacturers to take preventive action before costly breakdowns occurred.

Outcome:

The startup was able to help clients reduce equipment

downtime by up to **30%**. By implementing a cost-effective, compact AI solution, AutoMend enabled small and medium-sized factories to access predictive maintenance technology that would have otherwise been too expensive or technically complex for them to implement.

---

5. Case Study: AI for Smart Healthcare Diagnosis in a Telemedicine Startup

Company: HealthLine, a telemedicine startup offering online consultations and diagnostics through an AI-powered platform.

Challenge:

HealthLine wanted to integrate AI-driven diagnostic tools to assist doctors in providing faster and more accurate diagnoses. However, due to cost constraints and the need to ensure the AI model could run smoothly on mobile devices for accessibility, HealthLine was looking for compact AI solutions that could operate on a variety of devices with limited resources.

Solution:

HealthLine deployed a **small language model** trained to interpret patient symptoms, medical history, and basic diagnostic information in order to provide initial diagnoses and recommendations for further tests or treatments. The compact AI model was integrated into their mobile application, allowing patients to use the service on low-end smartphones.

- The small language model used **quantization** to reduce the computational resources required, while still maintaining accuracy in medical assessments.
- Integration with telemedicine systems allowed the model to assist doctors by providing recommendations during consultations, reducing

the time needed for diagnosis.

Outcome:

HealthLine saw a **40% reduction in diagnosis time** and enhanced user satisfaction as patients received faster feedback from doctors. The compact AI model played a key role in making telemedicine services more affordable and efficient, providing a valuable tool for startups targeting underserved populations.

Conclusion: Compact AI's Impact on Startups

These case studies illustrate how **compact AI models** are transforming startups by enabling them to access powerful, cost-effective AI tools that were once reserved for larger organizations. From customer support automation and personalized e-commerce experiences to fraud detection and predictive maintenance, compact AI is enabling startups to scale faster, reduce costs, and innovate within their industries. As the technology continues to evolve, we can expect even more success stories that demonstrate how small AI models can have **big impacts**, even for the smallest players in the market.

CASE STUDIES AND SUCCESS STORIES: INDUSTRY LEADERS ADOPTING SMALL MODELS

The adoption of small models is gaining momentum across industries, as leading companies recognize the significant benefits of using compact AI. These benefits include cost-effectiveness, energy efficiency, and faster deployment, all of which are essential for maintaining a competitive edge in today's fast-paced business environment. This chapter explores various **case studies and success stories** of industry leaders who have embraced small AI models to enhance their operations, reduce costs, and drive innovation.

---

1. Case Study: Compact AI for Real-Time Customer Insights in Retail - Walmart

Company: Walmart, the world's largest retailer, known for its wide range of consumer goods.

Challenge:

Walmart sought to enhance its customer experience by delivering personalized shopping experiences in real-time, using customer data collected across its vast retail network.

However, with millions of customers and vast amounts of data, traditional large-scale AI models were not feasible due to their computational cost and infrastructure demands.

Solution:

Walmart turned to **small language models** to deliver insights into customer preferences and behavior more efficiently. The company employed lightweight AI models to process customer interaction data and personalize product recommendations, promotions, and shopping experiences in real-time on both its website and in-store applications.

- By using **model distillation** and **quantization**, Walmart optimized its AI systems to deliver relevant insights with minimal computational power, allowing the models to be deployed directly on edge devices in stores and on its e-commerce platforms.

Outcome:

Walmart achieved a **30% increase in conversion rates** for personalized product recommendations while reducing the computational cost of AI operations. The implementation of small AI models allowed the retail giant to scale personalization services across its millions of customers without the need for expensive, cloud-based computing resources.

---

2. Case Study: AI for Fraud Detection in Banking - HSBC

Company: HSBC, a global leader in banking and financial services.

Challenge:

Fraud detection is a critical issue in the financial services industry. HSBC needed to process vast amounts of transaction data in real-time to identify fraudulent activities without relying on large-scale AI models that would require expensive infrastructure and storage.

Solution:

HSBC adopted **small AI models** designed for fraud detection. These models used **pruning techniques** to reduce the size of traditional fraud-detection algorithms while maintaining high accuracy. By deploying these compact models on edge devices, HSBC was able to provide real-time alerts to customers and flag potentially fraudulent transactions instantly.

- The **compressed AI models** were optimized for low-power systems, enabling efficient operation without cloud dependency.

Outcome:

HSBC was able to reduce false positives by **50%** and cut down processing times for detecting fraudulent activities by **40%**. With small AI models, HSBC successfully improved its fraud detection capabilities while lowering operational costs.

---

3. Case Study: Compact AI for Predictive Maintenance in Automotive - Tesla

Company: Tesla, a leader in electric vehicles and energy solutions.

Challenge:

Tesla aims to improve the efficiency of its production and vehicle performance by predicting maintenance needs for both its factory equipment and vehicles. The company needed an AI solution that could run in real-time on onboard systems and factory machines while managing large-scale data.

Solution:

Tesla integrated **small, compact AI models** for predictive maintenance in both its vehicles and manufacturing equipment. These models analyzed real-time data from vehicle sensors and factory machines to predict potential failures and maintenance requirements, ensuring vehicles stayed on the road and factories ran smoothly.

- **Quantization and distillation techniques** were employed to reduce the size and power consumption of the AI models, enabling them to be deployed directly on vehicle onboard systems and factory edge devices.

Outcome:

Tesla achieved a **20% reduction in unplanned maintenance** and a **15% improvement in vehicle uptime** by leveraging small AI models for predictive maintenance. This compact solution helped Tesla avoid costly repairs and increase the longevity of its fleet while keeping costs down.

---

4. Case Study: Compact AI for Voice Recognition in Smart Devices - Amazon

Company: Amazon, the global e-commerce and cloud computing giant, known for its voice assistant technology, Alexa.

Challenge:

Amazon wanted to improve the **voice recognition capabilities** of its Alexa smart devices, enabling users to interact naturally with technology. However, running large-scale voice models on devices with limited processing power presented significant challenges, especially for real-time voice recognition.

Solution:

Amazon adopted **small language models** for voice recognition in Alexa devices. By utilizing **model compression techniques**, Amazon reduced the size of the language models while maintaining accuracy and real-time response capabilities. These models were optimized to run directly on edge devices like Echo smart speakers.

- **Pruning and quantization** enabled the models to be more computationally efficient, allowing faster response times and more reliable voice recognition, even in noisy environments.

Outcome:

The implementation of compact AI models led to **faster voice recognition** and a **20% improvement in user satisfaction** for Alexa. By using smaller models, Amazon successfully improved the performance of its smart devices while keeping costs low and reducing energy consumption.

---

5. Case Study: AI for Smart Manufacturing in Electronics - Siemens

Company: Siemens, a global leader in automation and digitalization in manufacturing.

Challenge:

Siemens aimed to introduce **smart manufacturing** capabilities into its factories to optimize production lines and reduce energy consumption. The challenge was integrating AI models that could analyze sensor data and provide insights in real-time without overwhelming factory systems with large, resource-intensive models.

Solution:

Siemens leveraged **small AI models** for real-time process optimization and predictive maintenance on its production lines. These compact models were able to analyze data from sensors and predict potential equipment failures or inefficiencies without the need for large, complex AI models that required expensive computing resources.

- The models were deployed on **edge devices** and used **distillation** techniques to maintain accuracy while reducing their size and computational cost.

Outcome:

Siemens saw a **10% increase in production efficiency** and a

25% reduction in maintenance costs. The use of small AI models allowed Siemens to achieve high levels of automation and predictive insights while keeping hardware costs down.

---

6. Case Study: Small AI in Healthcare Diagnostics - Philips Healthcare

Company: Philips Healthcare, a leading global healthcare technology company.

Challenge:

Philips Healthcare wanted to integrate **AI-powered diagnostic tools** into medical devices to assist healthcare professionals in diagnosing diseases like cancer, heart conditions, and neurological disorders. The models needed to be fast and accurate but had to run on devices with limited computing power, such as portable ultrasound machines and mobile diagnostic systems.

Solution:

Philips deployed **small AI models** that utilized **pruning and quantization** techniques for enhanced speed and efficiency. These models analyzed patient data, such as ultrasound images and ECG results, in real-time to provide instant diagnostic feedback.

- The compact AI models were designed to work seamlessly on mobile and portable devices, ensuring that doctors in remote or resource-limited environments could access the same advanced diagnostic capabilities as in large hospitals.

Outcome:

Philips Healthcare saw a **40% improvement in diagnostic speed** and a **15% increase in diagnostic accuracy**, helping doctors provide faster, more accurate results for patients in remote locations. The compact AI models made high-quality diagnostics more accessible and affordable.

---

7. Case Study: AI for Personalized Learning in Education - Duolingo

Company: Duolingo, a language-learning platform that offers personalized lessons for users worldwide.

Challenge:

Duolingo needed to provide **personalized learning experiences** for millions of users, while ensuring that the language models behind its lesson recommendations were both efficient and scalable.

Solution:

Duolingo implemented **small language models** that were capable of generating personalized language-learning content based on individual user progress and performance. The models were optimized to run on mobile devices without requiring significant resources, ensuring a smooth user experience even on lower-end devices.

- **Model distillation** was used to ensure that the models were both small in size and fast in processing user data for real-time feedback.

Outcome:

Duolingo's use of small AI models resulted in a **25% improvement in user retention** and a more engaging learning experience for its users. The adoption of compact AI models helped Duolingo scale its services to millions of users across the globe without the need for expensive infrastructure.

Conclusion: Industry Leaders Pioneering Compact AI Adoption

These case studies demonstrate how **industry leaders** are adopting small models to solve complex challenges while maintaining operational efficiency. Whether in retail, finance, healthcare, manufacturing, or education, the benefits of compact AI models—such as cost savings, energy efficiency, and rapid deployment—are transforming industries and driving innovation. As technology continues to advance, small AI models will play an even more crucial role in shaping the future of global enterprises.

CASE STUDIES AND SUCCESS STORIES: COMMUNITY-DRIVEN AI INNOVATIONS

Community-driven AI innovations emphasize the power of collaboration, grassroots involvement, and shared knowledge in building solutions that address diverse challenges. By leveraging the expertise and creativity of global communities, these projects have successfully delivered cutting-edge AI applications, from health to social good, all while remaining resource-efficient and scalable. This chapter highlights several **community-driven AI innovations** that exemplify how AI can be used to drive meaningful, impactful change across industries and societies.

---

1. Case Study: AI for Conservation Efforts - Wildbook

Project: Wildbook, an open-source AI-powered platform for wildlife conservation.

Challenge:

Tracking and identifying endangered wildlife species is a complex task that requires vast amounts of data. Conservationists often struggle to track animals in remote areas and in large, diverse ecosystems, making it difficult to assess population health and plan effective protection measures.

Solution:

The **Wildbook community** built an AI system that uses **computer vision** and **machine learning** to identify and track animals by their unique markings (e.g., spots on a giraffe or patterns on a whale's tail). The community crowdsourced image data from wildlife photographers, citizen scientists, and researchers worldwide. These images were then fed into the AI model to train it to recognize individual animals.

- The project utilizes **small, lightweight AI models** to analyze images efficiently on low-resource devices in the field, enabling real-time monitoring and population tracking.

Outcome:

Wildbook has been successfully used to track hundreds of thousands of animals across multiple species. The platform's community-driven approach has led to **faster conservation efforts**, with over **70,000 individual animals** being tracked globally. Additionally, the system's ability to run on small devices in remote locations has greatly enhanced conservationists' ability to collect and analyze data without relying on powerful, centralized systems.

---

2. Case Study: Open-Source AI for Public Health - COVID-19 Open Research Dataset (CORD-19)

Project: CORD-19 (COVID-19 Open Research Dataset)

Challenge:

The onset of the COVID-19 pandemic created an urgent need for research and actionable insights related to the virus. A critical challenge was managing the rapidly growing amount of scientific literature and making it accessible to researchers around the world, so that effective public health interventions could be developed.

Solution:

The **CORD-19 project** was an open-source initiative spearheaded by a community of researchers, technologists, and institutions, including Microsoft, the Allen Institute for AI, and the National Institutes of Health (NIH). The project provided an AI-powered platform that made over **200,000 research papers** related to COVID-19 accessible, searchable, and usable for scientists and public health experts.

- **Small AI models** were used to **automate text mining** and **knowledge extraction**, helping researchers quickly sift through vast amounts of literature to identify patterns, potential drug candidates, and strategies for tackling the pandemic.

Outcome:

CORD-19 accelerated the global response to COVID-19 by facilitating collaborative research. The platform enabled thousands of researchers to make faster connections between scientific findings, leading to breakthroughs in areas such as drug repurposing, vaccine development, and disease modeling. The community-driven approach ensured that even researchers with limited access to computing resources could participate in and benefit from the project.

---

3. Case Study: AI for Disaster Response - OpenAI's Open Emergency Response Systems

Project: Open Emergency Response Systems

Challenge:

Disaster response teams face critical challenges in processing large volumes of data in real-time, especially in the aftermath of natural disasters like hurricanes, earthquakes, or floods. Information about the affected areas needs to be collected, analyzed, and acted upon swiftly to minimize casualties and aid recovery efforts.

Solution:

A collaborative, **community-driven AI project** called **Open Emergency Response Systems** was launched to improve the efficiency of disaster management. The system aggregates data from multiple sources, including social media, satellite imagery, and emergency services, and processes it using **AI-powered algorithms** for damage assessment, resource allocation, and real-time communication.

- **Small AI models** running on low-cost devices and **edge computing** resources were used for initial data processing, reducing the need for expensive infrastructure and ensuring that insights could be delivered quickly and effectively.

Outcome:

The Open Emergency Response Systems helped reduce response times by **30%** and improved the efficiency of aid delivery in regions hit by disasters. The community-driven collaboration allowed small, underfunded organizations to leverage cutting-edge AI technology and significantly improve disaster preparedness and recovery efforts.

---

4. Case Study: AI for Agriculture - FarmBot

Project: FarmBot, an open-source precision farming robot.

Challenge:

Agricultural practices face growing challenges, including climate change, soil depletion, and the need to feed an expanding global population. Smallholder farmers, especially in low-resource settings, struggle to access technology that can help them optimize crop yields and reduce environmental impact.

Solution:

The **FarmBot community** developed an open-source, AI-powered robotic system designed to help farmers automate planting, watering, and tending to crops in a precise and environmentally sustainable manner. The robot uses a combination of **machine learning**, **computer vision**, and **edge AI** to monitor crops, detect pests, and optimize irrigation.

- By using **small, energy-efficient AI models**, FarmBot can operate on low-power devices, making it accessible to small farmers with limited access to energy and computing resources.

Outcome:

FarmBot has been successfully implemented in over **25 countries**. The robot has helped farmers increase yields by **40%** while reducing water usage by up to **60%**. Its open-source model has empowered a global community of farmers, researchers, and technologists to adapt the system to different agricultural conditions, driving innovation in sustainable farming.

---

5. Case Study: AI for Education - Khan Academy's AI-Powered Learning Assistant

Project: Khan Academy's AI Learning Assistant

Challenge:

Access to quality education remains a significant challenge in many regions of the world, particularly in rural and underserved communities. Personalized learning at scale requires extensive resources, including highly trained educators, which can be difficult to provide in these areas.

Solution:

Khan Academy, a non-profit educational platform, incorporated **small AI models** into its learning platform to create a **personalized AI-powered learning assistant** for students. The system uses AI to track each student's progress and provide customized feedback, recommendations, and practice exercises.

- The system was designed to run efficiently on low-cost, mobile-friendly devices to ensure accessibility in underprivileged regions with limited infrastructure.

Outcome:

Khan Academy's AI-powered assistant has enabled **millions of students** around the world to receive personalized education. In regions with scarce educational resources, students using the platform have shown a **50% improvement** in math and reading proficiency. The community-driven, open-source nature of the platform has allowed teachers and students to customize learning paths, making education more inclusive and equitable.

---

6. Case Study: AI for Social Good - DataKind

Project: DataKind, a nonprofit organization connecting data scientists with social impact organizations.

Challenge:

Nonprofits and social impact organizations often lack the technical expertise and resources to leverage AI and data science for solving complex social challenges, such as poverty, inequality, and climate change.

Solution:

DataKind is a community-driven initiative that connects skilled data scientists with nonprofit organizations to develop AI solutions for social good. Through collaborations, DataKind has helped create AI-powered tools for **predicting homelessness**, **optimizing food distribution**, and **improving disaster response**.

- The community-driven model allows data scientists to volunteer their expertise to develop solutions for organizations working in fields with limited access to resources.

Outcome:

DataKind has empowered over **200 social impact organizations** worldwide, resulting in the development of over **30 AI-powered solutions** for social good. Their efforts have led to **improved targeting of resources** for homeless shelters, better food distribution models, and more efficient humanitarian responses during crises.

Conclusion: Empowering Communities with Compact AI Solutions

These community-driven AI innovations show the profound impact that collaboration, open-source technology, and compact AI models can have on a global scale. By leveraging the collective efforts of diverse communities and providing accessible, low-resource solutions, these projects address some of the world's most pressing challenges, from wildlife conservation to social good. As small AI models continue to evolve, their role in empowering communities to drive meaningful change will only expand, creating opportunities for innovation in every corner of the world.

CHALLENGES AND LIMITATIONS: BALANCING ACCURACY WITH SIZE

One of the primary challenges in developing **small language models (SLMs)** is achieving an optimal balance between the model's **accuracy** and its **size**. Smaller models are highly efficient in terms of resource usage, but they often face trade-offs in performance, which can impact their effectiveness across different tasks. Striking the right balance is crucial for ensuring that small models can provide valuable insights and functionality without being overburdened by unnecessary computational overhead. Here's a breakdown of the challenges and limitations involved in balancing **accuracy** with **size** in compact AI models:

---

1. Reduced Model Capacity

- **Challenge:** Smaller models have fewer parameters and less computational capacity compared to their larger counterparts. This reduction in parameters can lead to a **loss of representational power**, which is essential for capturing the complexity of language, nuances in meaning, and subtle patterns in data.
- **Impact:** This can result in **lower performance** on complex tasks, such as **natural language**

understanding (NLU), **contextual generation**, and **fine-grained sentiment analysis**, where large models like GPT or BERT typically excel. Smaller models might not be able to handle tasks requiring deep contextual awareness, making them less accurate in specific applications.

---

2. Overfitting vs. Underfitting

- **Challenge:** In the case of small models, there's a **risk of underfitting** the data, where the model is too simple to capture the underlying patterns, leading to **poor generalization** and inaccurate results. Conversely, **overfitting** can also occur when small models are trained excessively on limited data, resulting in **over-specialization** to that data set and poor performance on unseen data.
- **Impact:** A model that underfits may fail to make accurate predictions or provide useful outputs, while one that overfits may struggle to generalize to different contexts. Balancing these tendencies is crucial to improving the model's real-world utility.

---

3. Trade-offs Between Speed and Accuracy

- **Challenge:** Small language models are typically optimized for speed and resource efficiency, especially in real-time applications such as **edge computing** or **mobile devices**. However, this optimization often comes at the cost of accuracy, as reducing the model size can involve compressing the model to a degree that results in less precision.
- **Impact:** This can be particularly problematic for applications requiring high accuracy, such as **medical diagnosis**, **legal analysis**, or **financial forecasting**, where even a small loss in accuracy can

lead to significant negative consequences. Ensuring that the model maintains an acceptable level of performance without sacrificing efficiency is a delicate balancing act.

---

4. Generalization Challenges

- **Challenge:** Small models, due to their reduced size, often struggle with generalization—applying knowledge learned in one context to new, unseen situations. They may perform well on a specific set of training data but fail when exposed to **diverse data** or **new contexts**.
- **Impact:** The inability to generalize across diverse tasks or datasets means that compact models may not be as versatile as larger models, which benefit from larger training datasets and more complex architectures that allow them to learn and adapt across various domains.

---

5. Compression Techniques and Their Limits

- **Challenge:** Techniques such as **model pruning**, **quantization**, and **distillation** are commonly used to reduce the size of large models. However, these techniques have inherent limitations. For instance, **pruning** removes less important weights, which might also remove critical components of the model's decision-making process. **Quantization** reduces the precision of numbers representing weights, which could affect the model's ability to represent subtle variations in data.
- **Impact:** These techniques often lead to a **trade-off between performance and efficiency**. While they can dramatically reduce model size and improve inference time, they can also lead to a **drop in**

accuracy, particularly in tasks that require precision or involve ambiguous, complex input data.

---

6. Domain-Specific Challenges

- **Challenge:** Small language models are more vulnerable to **domain-specific limitations**, where accuracy is highly dependent on the context or field of application. For example, a small model trained on general language data may struggle with specialized jargon or context-specific language found in fields like **law**, **medicine**, or **engineering**.
- **Impact:** Inaccurate results in specialized domains could undermine the model's usefulness in practical applications, making it less reliable for professional or industrial tasks. Balancing the need for compactness with the ability to perform effectively in niche domains is a key challenge.

---

7. Fine-Tuning and Transfer Learning

- **Challenge:** While larger models can often be fine-tuned to perform specific tasks by training them on task-specific datasets, small models may have limited capacity for **fine-tuning** without drastically affecting their performance. Fine-tuning a small model on specialized data can lead to issues like **catastrophic forgetting**, where the model loses generalization ability in favor of task-specific performance.
- **Impact:** Small models might require frequent retraining to maintain performance across a variety of tasks, leading to inefficiencies. Moreover, the challenge of retaining general knowledge while becoming task-specific can limit the model's flexibility and adaptability.

8. Handling Complex Tasks

- **Challenge:** Many complex tasks, such as **question answering, conversational AI**, or **multimodal inputs** (combining text, images, and speech), require high levels of **contextual reasoning** and **multi-step inference**. Small models, with their limited capacity, may struggle to process these tasks effectively.
- **Impact:** The reduction in model size means there are fewer mechanisms available for capturing long-term dependencies or handling intricate tasks, which can lead to significant accuracy degradation in such scenarios.

9. Evaluation Metrics and Benchmarks

- **Challenge:** Smaller models may exhibit **satisfactory performance** on certain benchmarks but fail to deliver when evaluated in real-world scenarios or on complex tasks. The traditional evaluation metrics may not fully capture the trade-offs between **speed, size, and accuracy** that matter for specific applications.
- **Impact:** Without more holistic, context-driven metrics that account for the broader use case, small models might appear more effective in controlled environments than they truly are when deployed in dynamic, real-world settings.

10. Long-Term Viability

- **Challenge:** The long-term viability of small models is still a subject of debate. As computational power increases and larger models continue to improve, the **advantages of small models** in terms of efficiency and speed might become less significant.

Furthermore, advancements in **distributed computing** or **quantum computing** could render the trade-off between size and performance less critical.

- **Impact:** While compact models have their niche in resource-constrained environments, there is uncertainty about their ability to keep up with the increasing complexity of tasks and the growing need for even larger, more sophisticated models.

Conclusion

The balancing act between **accuracy** and **size** is one of the most pressing challenges in the development and deployment of small language models. Achieving this balance requires **innovative techniques** in model compression, **careful attention** to task requirements, and **continuous research** into optimizing small models for both performance and efficiency. Understanding these challenges is crucial for developing compact AI solutions that deliver value across a wide range of applications while maintaining robustness, scalability, and real-world utility.

CHALLENGES AND LIMITATIONS: NAVIGATING THE COMPUTATIONAL LIMITS

As small language models (SLMs) become increasingly important for various real-time and resource-constrained applications, one of the key obstacles is navigating the **computational limits** inherent in these models. While small models are celebrated for their efficiency, portability, and ability to run on edge devices, they still face significant challenges in terms of computational constraints, which impact their performance, scalability, and adaptability. Here are the key challenges and limitations in **navigating computational limits** when working with small AI models:

---

1. Memory and Storage Constraints

- **Challenge:** Small models are designed to be **memory-efficient** by reducing the number of parameters and the overall computational footprint. However, even compact models require careful management of memory and storage, especially when deployed on **mobile devices**, **IoT systems**, or **edge computing environments** with limited resources.

- **Impact:** Running a model with a large dataset in real-time can overwhelm the available memory, leading to **slower inference times**, increased **latency**, or even system crashes. Limited storage also restricts the ability to store large, pre-trained models or task-specific data, limiting flexibility.

---

2. Reduced Model Complexity vs. Performance Trade-offs

- **Challenge:** To meet computational constraints, small models are intentionally designed with fewer parameters, fewer layers, or **simplified architectures**. While this enhances efficiency, it reduces the model's **capacity for learning** from complex data, limiting its **expressive power**.
- **Impact:** This leads to trade-offs in performance, as small models may struggle to handle tasks that require **deep contextual understanding** or **fine-grained decision-making**. For example, tasks involving **multi-step reasoning**, **ambiguous language processing**, or **advanced pattern recognition** may see significant performance degradation in small models.

---

3. Speed vs. Accuracy Dilemma

- **Challenge:** Small models excel in scenarios requiring **fast processing** due to their reduced size, making them ideal candidates for applications such as **real-time language translation**, **speech recognition**, or **chatbots**. However, achieving high speed often comes at the expense of **accuracy**, as smaller models have a limited ability to capture subtle nuances and complex language structures.
- **Impact:** While small models can deliver quick outputs, they may produce **less accurate** or **less**

coherent results when compared to their larger counterparts. This is particularly evident in tasks requiring **high precision**, like medical diagnosis or legal document analysis, where even small errors could lead to significant consequences.

---

4. Inference Latency in Real-Time Applications

- **Challenge: Inference latency**—the time it takes for a model to process input data and return a prediction—is a critical performance metric in many applications. Small models are often deployed in environments that require low-latency predictions, such as **real-time decision-making** systems, **autonomous vehicles**, or **voice assistants**.
- **Impact:** Despite being compact, small models may still face challenges in meeting the ultra-low latency requirements of certain applications, particularly when the task demands real-time updates, as in **financial trading** or **medical monitoring**. This can lead to a **lag in response times**, affecting the user experience and real-time decision-making processes.

---

5. Scalability Issues in Complex Tasks

- **Challenge:** While small models are highly optimized for specific tasks and can scale well in many edge scenarios, they often struggle to **scale** effectively when faced with more complex or **multimodal tasks**. For instance, tasks such as **multimodal fusion** (combining text, images, and sound) or **advanced question answering** require intricate **inter-model interactions** that small models may not handle as efficiently.
- **Impact:** Small models might **fail to generalize** across a wide range of use cases, making them

less adaptable in real-world environments where dynamic, evolving data is common. Their limited capacity for handling **large-scale** or **cross-domain tasks** leads to **poor scalability**, especially in enterprise or industrial applications that demand versatility.

---

6. Difficulty in Handling Diverse Data Types

- **Challenge:** Small models are designed with limited computational resources in mind, which makes them well-suited for tasks where the input data is relatively homogeneous or simple. However, when faced with **diverse data types**—for example, a mixture of **text, audio, and visual data**—small models may struggle to process and integrate this complex information efficiently.
- **Impact:** This limitation makes it difficult for small models to effectively handle **multimodal applications**, such as **video analysis**, **speech-to-text conversion**, or **autonomous systems**. Consequently, these models may perform poorly in domains requiring integration across multiple input modalities, limiting their effectiveness in advanced AI systems.

---

7. Limited Parallelization and Hardware Utilization

- **Challenge:** Small models are often **optimized for deployment on single processors** or edge devices with limited parallel processing capabilities. While they may be efficient in these scenarios, their reduced capacity for parallelization can hinder performance in high-demand, distributed environments.
- **Impact:** This limitation means that small models may fail to take full advantage of **multi-**

core processors, GPU acceleration, or cloud-based resources—all of which are essential for scaling AI models in large, distributed systems. In tasks requiring heavy computational demands, the inability to distribute the load effectively can severely limit the model's efficiency and speed.

---

8. Lack of Fine-Grained Control Over Inference Process

- **Challenge:** Many small models rely on **pre-defined architectures** with limited configurability or flexibility. This means that there is **less room for fine-tuning** or **adjusting** the inference process based on specific operational needs.
- **Impact:** As a result, small models often operate in a **one-size-fits-all** manner, where optimization for one use case (e.g., speed) might lead to inefficiencies in others (e.g., accuracy). For instance, a model optimized for speed in a mobile app might sacrifice nuanced output for the sake of responsiveness, making it less effective for specific, context-dependent applications.

---

9. Lack of Robustness in Adverse Conditions

- **Challenge:** Smaller models, due to their simplicity, may not have the **robustness** needed to perform well in **adverse or uncertain conditions**, such as noisy data, ambiguous language, or low-quality inputs.
- **Impact:** In environments where data is imperfect, such as real-time audio streams or **crowdsourced text inputs**, the lack of sophistication in smaller models can lead to **high error rates**, reducing their reliability. Models may struggle to handle edge cases or rare events, leading to **inconsistent performance** in challenging real-world scenarios.

10. Cost of Frequent Updates and Maintenance

- **Challenge:** Small models may require frequent updates to ensure that they remain **relevant** and **accurate** in evolving environments. However, the **maintenance cost** of updating models on edge devices, especially those that need to operate without a constant internet connection, can be high. Additionally, retraining small models on fresh data or incorporating **new algorithms** can strain computational resources.
- **Impact:** The inability to keep the models continuously updated can make them less effective in dynamic environments, where models need to adapt to changing patterns or newly available data. The cost and logistical challenges of frequent updates can reduce the model's long-term usability, especially in applications that require high levels of accuracy.

Conclusion

Navigating the computational limits of small language models presents a multifaceted challenge. While small models offer significant advantages in efficiency, portability, and speed, they must overcome trade-offs in terms of memory, complexity, scalability, and robustness. To fully realize the potential of compact AI in real-world applications, it's essential to continue improving techniques for overcoming these limitations, ensuring that small models remain adaptable, efficient, and capable of delivering high-quality results even under computational constraints.

CHALLENGES AND LIMITATIONS: ETHICAL AND SOCIETAL IMPLICATIONS

As the use of small language models (SLMs) and compact AI technologies grows, there are increasing concerns about the **ethical** and **societal** implications of deploying these models in real-world applications. While these models promise efficiency, accessibility, and innovation, they also bring challenges that require careful consideration, especially in areas like **bias, privacy, accountability**, and **impact on jobs**. Below are the key ethical and societal challenges that arise when working with small language models:

---

1. Bias and Fairness in Small Models

- **Challenge:** Small language models, like larger ones, are often trained on vast amounts of text data sourced from the internet, books, and other publicly available repositories. These datasets may contain **cultural, racial, gender, or socio-economic biases**, which can inadvertently be reflected in the model's outputs. As these models are deployed in real-world applications, they can perpetuate or even amplify these biases, especially when working with data that is not sufficiently diverse or balanced.

- **Impact:** Bias in small models can lead to **unfair treatment**, especially in sensitive domains like **recruitment**, **healthcare diagnostics**, **law enforcement**, and **financial services**, where biased decisions can have significant consequences for individuals or communities. For example, biased language models could produce inaccurate job recommendations, discriminatory loan approvals, or biased legal rulings.

---

2. Transparency and Explainability

- **Challenge:** Small models, by their very nature, are **designed to be compact and efficient**, often trading off interpretability for speed and performance. However, as these models are increasingly used in critical domains such as **medical diagnoses**, **legal advice**, and **financial decisions**, there is a growing demand for **transparency** and **explainability** in AI systems.
- **Impact:** The lack of **transparency** in how small models arrive at decisions can raise ethical concerns, particularly when models are used to make decisions that directly affect individuals' lives. **Non-explainable decisions** could undermine **trust** in AI, making it difficult for users to understand why a particular decision was made or to contest those decisions if necessary.

---

3. Data Privacy and Security

- **Challenge:** Small models, particularly those deployed on edge devices or mobile applications, process data locally rather than sending it to a central server.

While this can improve **data privacy** by reducing the amount of sensitive information transmitted, it also poses challenges for ensuring the **security** of user data. Many small models operate in environments where **data collection** is continuous, and without proper safeguards, they can inadvertently leak personal or sensitive information.

- **Impact:** Small models processing user data on devices like smartphones, wearables, or voice assistants could lead to **privacy violations** or **data misuse** if not properly secured. **Hackers** may exploit vulnerabilities in these models, especially when they are not subjected to rigorous testing or updating. Moreover, the growing amount of personal data generated through AI interactions could be vulnerable to misuse or theft, violating users' privacy rights.

---

4. Accountability and Liability

- **Challenge:** As small language models are increasingly adopted in sectors where they influence critical decisions (e.g., healthcare, finance, or law enforcement), questions of **accountability** and **liability** arise. When a small model makes a wrong decision—whether it's a misdiagnosis, a denied loan, or a faulty recommendation—who is responsible for the consequences?
- **Impact:** The **lack of accountability** in small model-based systems could lead to **legal and ethical dilemmas**. If an error occurs due to an **algorithmic decision**, it might be unclear whether the responsibility lies with the **developers**, the **organizations** that deployed the system, or the **AI model itself**. This could result in a lack of recourse for individuals affected by these decisions, especially

when there is no clear framework for addressing grievances.

---

5. Job Displacement and Economic Inequality

- **Challenge:** While small language models are designed to automate many tasks, from customer service to content moderation, there are concerns about their role in **job displacement**. As these models automate repetitive and low-skill tasks, they may reduce the need for human labor in certain industries, leading to **unemployment** and economic inequality, particularly in **low-wage** sectors.
- **Impact:** The deployment of small models may disproportionately affect vulnerable workers who perform **routine, manual jobs**. If these individuals are unable to transition to more complex roles or retrain in areas less susceptible to automation, it could exacerbate **social inequality** and **economic divides**. Additionally, as automation accelerates, there may be growing concerns about a **digital divide** where only those with access to advanced technologies and the skills to use them benefit from the AI revolution.

---

6. Ethical Use of Personal Data

- **Challenge:** Small models used for tasks like **customer service**, **personal assistants**, and **healthcare applications** often require access to vast amounts of personal data to function effectively. While these models can improve user experiences by offering personalized recommendations or better service, the ethical use of this data remains a critical concern.
- **Impact:** If personal data is not handled responsibly, it can lead to **violations of trust**, especially if data

is used for purposes other than originally intended. Furthermore, the **collection**, **storage**, and **sharing** of personal data could lead to the exploitation of individuals' information for **advertising**, **surveillance**, or even **political manipulation** without the user's consent.

---

7. Accessibility and Inclusion

- **Challenge:** While small models can increase access to AI-powered technologies in **low-resource** settings, there is a risk that they might only serve **privileged populations** if not implemented thoughtfully. Limited access to high-speed internet, adequate hardware, or digital literacy in **developing countries** could result in a **widening digital divide**, where the benefits of small AI models are concentrated among certain groups.
- **Impact:** Without proper attention to **accessibility**, small models could inadvertently marginalize communities in **low-income regions** or **underrepresented groups**. This could limit the equitable benefits of AI and exacerbate social inequality. For example, if small language models are used for educational purposes but are only available in high-income countries with robust digital infrastructure, they could further entrench educational disparities.

---

8. Misinformation and Disinformation

- **Challenge:** Small language models can be **used to generate content** such as news articles, social media posts, or even fake reviews. This can be a double-edged sword—while it can create efficiencies and enable scalable communication, it also raises concerns about **misinformation** and **disinformation**.

- **Impact:** If small models are not properly regulated or monitored, they could be exploited by malicious actors to generate **false narratives**, **manipulate public opinion**, or **undermine trust in institutions**. This is especially problematic in **political contexts**, where disinformation can have serious consequences on elections or public policies.

---

9. Environmental Impact

- **Challenge:** Even though small models are designed to be more **energy-efficient** than larger models, they still require computational resources, particularly during the training phase. Training models on large datasets and maintaining them on distributed systems can contribute to a significant **carbon footprint**.
- **Impact:** The deployment of small models across various industries and applications could still add to the **environmental burden** if proper sustainability measures aren't taken. For example, training these models on energy-intensive data centers can have a considerable **environmental impact** if the infrastructure is not **green** or powered by **renewable energy** sources.

---

10. Ethical Standards and Regulation

- **Challenge:** As small models become widely used, there is a growing need for consistent **ethical standards** and **regulatory frameworks** that govern their development and deployment. The **global nature** of AI technology poses challenges in creating universally accepted standards for ethics and fairness.

- **Impact:** Without effective governance, the ethical implications of small AI models could vary widely across different regions, sectors, or applications. A lack of clear regulation could lead to unethical practices, such as **exploitation of vulnerable users** or the **development of harmful AI systems**. As a result, countries or companies that do not adhere to **ethical principles** may exploit these gaps, undermining the positive potential of small language models.

Conclusion

While small language models bring immense potential in terms of efficiency, accessibility, and real-world applications, their deployment raises significant **ethical** and **societal** concerns. Addressing these challenges requires a multi-faceted approach, including promoting **transparency**, mitigating **bias**, ensuring **data privacy**, and developing frameworks for **accountability**. Only by confronting these ethical dilemmas head-on can small models be used responsibly and equitably to foster innovation while minimizing harm.

REFLECTING ON THE IMPACT OF COMPACT AI

The emergence of compact AI models, especially in the form of small language models (SLMs), has transformed a range of industries, from healthcare and education to finance and customer service. These models—characterized by their efficiency, low computational requirements, and versatility—are shaping how artificial intelligence (AI) can be integrated into daily life. As we reflect on their impact, it is essential to consider both the **positive transformations** they are driving and the **challenges** they present. The impact of compact AI is multifaceted, affecting **technological innovation**, **business models**, **societal structures**, and even **ethical considerations**.

---

1. Empowering Accessibility and Efficiency

One of the most significant contributions of compact AI is its ability to make **advanced technologies accessible** to a broader range of people and industries. Small models, being lightweight and optimized for use in low-resource settings, democratize access to AI. They allow for the deployment of powerful tools on **smartphones**, **IoT devices**, and **wearables** —devices that are ubiquitous even in low-income and developing regions.

- **Impact on Everyday Users**: Compact models enable users in **emerging economies** to access

AI capabilities like language translation, medical advice, and financial services, helping to bridge the digital divide. For instance, rural communities in low-resource settings can now benefit from **mobile health solutions**, which can be used to detect diseases or advise on treatments.

- **Impact on Businesses**: Small models lower the cost of AI integration, enabling small and medium enterprises (SMEs) to implement AI-powered applications. This, in turn, leads to increased productivity, automation of routine tasks, and enhanced decision-making capabilities, all without the need for extensive infrastructure or high computational resources.

---

2. Driving Innovation Across Industries

Compact AI models are reshaping various industries by offering an efficient and scalable solution to AI challenges. They offer real-time, context-aware capabilities and are increasingly being adopted for use in consumer electronics, autonomous systems, healthcare, and more.

- **Healthcare**: Compact AI models have revolutionized diagnostics, especially in **low-resource healthcare settings** where access to advanced infrastructure and medical expertise is limited. AI-powered diagnostic tools, such as image recognition systems, are now able to operate on **mobile devices** in remote areas, providing vital health support in real-time.
- **Automotive and Smart Devices**: In the realm of **autonomous vehicles**, compact models assist in sensor fusion, object detection, and navigation systems without overwhelming on-board computing resources. Meanwhile, in **smart devices** like voice assistants and wearables, small models can enhance

user experience by offering fast, localized processing capabilities.

- **Customer Service and Retail**: AI-driven chatbots, powered by compact models, can now provide high-quality customer support across industries. This has significantly improved response times, customer satisfaction, and operational costs.

---

3. Enhancing Personalization and User Experience

Compact AI's real-time capabilities have enabled a leap forward in **personalized user experiences**. By using smaller models that can process data on-device, businesses and applications can offer highly relevant and individualized services. Whether it's recommending products, tailoring content, or providing customized healthcare advice, compact models bring AI-powered personalization to **every user** in an affordable, scalable manner.

- **E-commerce**: Small models can analyze user behavior to personalize product recommendations, significantly improving conversion rates and customer loyalty.
- **Social Media and Content Platforms**: Personalization of content feeds, news articles, and advertisements is increasingly powered by compact AI models, enhancing user engagement without the need to rely on resource-heavy cloud infrastructure.

---

4. Reducing Environmental Footprint

An often-overlooked impact of compact AI is its potential to reduce the **carbon footprint** of artificial intelligence. Larger AI models, particularly those in natural language processing and deep learning, require massive computational resources, contributing to **high energy consumption**. By contrast, small models require significantly less computational power, allowing for AI capabilities to be delivered without taxing energy resources.

- **Sustainability**: As global concerns about **climate change** and **sustainability** rise, compact AI offers a potential solution. AI models optimized for **energy efficiency** contribute to the larger global goal of reducing the environmental impact of technology. Compact models are particularly valuable in regions where **green energy** is a priority, as they help minimize the energy demand of data centers and other computational infrastructure.

---

5. Addressing Global Challenges

Compact AI plays an essential role in addressing **global challenges** such as **climate change**, **public health crises**, and **poverty**. In resource-constrained settings, compact models can help overcome barriers to **data collection**, **analysis**, and **action**.

- **Disaster Response**: Compact AI models, when integrated with **IoT sensors**, can help predict and monitor environmental conditions like floods, droughts, and wildfires, providing **real-time alerts** to mitigate damage in disaster-prone regions.
- **Agriculture**: Small AI models deployed in **smart farming technologies** can assist in analyzing soil health, optimizing irrigation, and predicting crop yields, helping farmers in developing countries improve their productivity and reduce waste.

---

6. Ethical and Societal Challenges

While compact AI brings tremendous benefits, it also raises several **ethical and societal concerns**. As AI becomes more embedded in everyday life, its implications go beyond technical limitations, touching upon areas like **privacy**, **bias**,

security, and **social equity**.

- **Bias and Fairness**: Like larger models, compact models can inherit biases from the data they are trained on. This could result in discriminatory outcomes, especially in areas like hiring, lending, and law enforcement. The challenge is to ensure that these models are **fair**, **transparent**, and **accountable**.
- **Privacy Concerns**: As compact models are deployed on personal devices, issues related to **data privacy** and **security** become critical. Users' personal data is often stored and processed locally, which can reduce the risk of exposure to large-scale breaches but also necessitates stricter protocols to ensure that sensitive information remains secure.
- **Job Displacement**: The growing automation capabilities of compact models could lead to the displacement of certain jobs, especially in sectors like customer service, retail, and low-skilled labor. While these models can improve productivity and reduce operational costs, they may also exacerbate issues related to **job loss** and **economic inequality**.

---

7. The Future of Compact AI

Looking ahead, the potential of compact AI is vast. The **advancement of model compression techniques**, **edge computing**, and **energy-efficient algorithms** will continue to drive its adoption and increase its impact. Moreover, as **multimodal models** evolve and small models become even more integrated into everyday devices, the possibilities for **personalized** and **scalable AI solutions** will expand, leading to even greater transformation across industries.

The **future of compact AI** will likely include **ubiquitous AI-driven technologies** that are highly integrated into **smart cities**, **automated manufacturing**, **precision healthcare**, and

sustainable agriculture, among others. As these models become more capable and accessible, they will continue to redefine how we interact with technology and tackle some of the world's most pressing challenges.

Conclusion

Compact AI is not just about creating smaller models; it's about unlocking **new possibilities** for efficiency, accessibility, and innovation across a wide range of sectors. By enhancing personalization, reducing energy consumption, and enabling widespread adoption, small models are laying the groundwork for a more connected and sustainable future. However, as with any technological advancement, there are important ethical, social, and economic considerations that need to be addressed to ensure that the benefits of compact AI are shared equitably and responsibly. As we move forward, the potential of compact AI to transform industries, improve lives, and drive global progress remains immense.

CASE STUDY: SMALL LANGUAGE MODEL FOR SENTIMENT ANALYSIS IN E-COMMERCE

Background:

A popular e-commerce platform wants to analyze customer reviews to extract sentiments and improve product recommendations. However, the platform faces constraints in terms of computational resources, especially because millions of reviews are generated daily. Large-scale sentiment analysis models would be too expensive and slow, so the platform decides to use a **small language model** optimized for sentiment classification.

The goal is to develop an AI model that can efficiently analyze customer reviews in real-time and classify them as positive, neutral, or negative. The solution should be able to run on edge devices like smartphones or low-resource servers in order to provide **low-latency** and **cost-effective** sentiment analysis.

Solution Approach:

We use a **small language model** fine-tuned for sentiment analysis, leveraging the Hugging Face transformers library and a pre-trained distilBERT model. DistilBERT is a distilled version of the larger BERT model that has fewer parameters, making it faster and more suitable for environments with limited computational resources.

Steps:

1. **Data Collection**: We collect a dataset of customer reviews along with sentiment labels (positive, neutral, negative).
2. **Model Selection**: We select distilBERT as the base model, which has been fine-tuned for sentiment analysis.
3. **Fine-tuning**: We fine-tune the model on our sentiment analysis dataset to improve its performance on e-commerce reviews.
4. **Deployment**: The model is deployed on edge devices to analyze incoming customer reviews in real-time.

Implementation Details

We will use the Hugging Face transformers library to load a pre-trained distilBERT model and fine-tune it for sentiment analysis on a sample e-commerce review dataset. Below is the code for training and deploying the model.

1. Installing Required Libraries

You will need to install the transformers and datasets libraries. You can do this via pip:

```
pip install transformers datasets torch
```

2. Loading and Preprocessing the Dataset

We will use a sample dataset of customer reviews and preprocess it to fine-tune the distilBERT model.

```
from datasets import load_dataset

from transformers import DistilBertTokenizerFast
```

```
# Load a sample sentiment analysis dataset (e.g., Amazon reviews dataset)
dataset = load_dataset("amazon_polarity")

# Load pre-trained tokenizer for distilBERT
tokenizer = DistilBertTokenizerFast.from_pretrained('distilbert-base-uncased')

# Preprocess the dataset to tokenize reviews
def tokenize_function(examples):
    return tokenizer(examples['text'], padding="max_length", truncation=True)

# Tokenize the training and testing datasets
tokenized_datasets = dataset.map(tokenize_function, batched=True)
```

3. Fine-tuning the Model

Next, we load a pre-trained distilBERT model, which is already fine-tuned for sentiment analysis tasks, and fine-tune it further on our dataset.

```
from transformers import DistilBertForSequenceClassification, Trainer, TrainingArguments
import torch

# Load the pre-trained distilBERT model with a classification head for sentiment analysis
model = DistilBertForSequenceClassification.from_pretrained('distilbe
```

```
rt-base-uncased', num_labels=2)

# Prepare the dataset for training
train_dataset = tokenized_datasets['train']
test_dataset = tokenized_datasets['test']

# Set up the training arguments
training_args = TrainingArguments(
    output_dir='./results',        # Output directory
    evaluation_strategy="epoch",   # Evaluate after every epoch
    learning_rate=2e-5,            # Learning rate
    per_device_train_batch_size=16,  # Batch size per device
during training
    per_device_eval_batch_size=16,   # Batch size per device
during evaluation
    num_train_epochs=3,            # Number of training epochs
    weight_decay=0.01,             # Strength of weight decay
)

# Initialize Trainer
trainer = Trainer(
    model=model,                   # The model to train
    args=training_args,            # The training arguments
    train_dataset=train_dataset,   # The training dataset
    eval_dataset=test_dataset      # The evaluation dataset
)

# Train the model
```

```
trainer.train()
```

4. Evaluating the Model

After training, you can evaluate the model's performance on the test set to check its accuracy.

```
# Evaluate the model
results = trainer.evaluate()

# Print the evaluation results
print(f"Test Results: {results}")
```

5. Making Predictions

Once the model is trained, you can use it to make predictions on new customer reviews.

```
# Function to predict sentiment for a new review
def predict_sentiment(review_text):
    inputs = tokenizer(review_text, return_tensors="pt", truncation=True, padding=True, max_length=512)
    outputs = model(inputs)
    logits = outputs.logits
    predicted_class = torch.argmax(logits, dim=-1).item()
    sentiment = "Positive" if predicted_class == 1 else "Negative"
    return sentiment

# Example of prediction
new_review = "I love this product! It works great and exceeded my expectations."
print(predict_sentiment(new_review))
```

Key Results and Impact

- **Real-time Sentiment Analysis**: The fine-tuned

model can classify the sentiment of reviews in real-time, providing instant feedback to e-commerce platforms for customer satisfaction tracking.

- **Resource Efficiency**: By using a **small language model** like distilBERT, the sentiment analysis process is computationally efficient, allowing the system to run on devices with lower processing power, such as smartphones or embedded systems.
- **Scalability**: The system can handle a large volume of reviews daily, making it suitable for large-scale e-commerce platforms that require efficient processing of customer feedback.

Conclusion

This case study demonstrates how compact AI, specifically small language models like distilBERT, can be used in real-world applications like sentiment analysis for e-commerce. These models provide a cost-effective, scalable, and efficient solution for tasks that typically require significant computational power. The model's ability to run on edge devices allows businesses to analyze customer feedback in real-time, providing actionable insights while maintaining low operational costs.

CASE STUDY: COMPACT AI FOR REAL-TIME LANGUAGE TRANSLATION IN MOBILE APPS

Background:

A mobile app development company aims to provide real-time language translation for users across multiple languages. The app is designed for international travelers who need quick and accurate translations for communication in various regions. Since the app will run on smartphones with limited resources (memory, storage, and processing power), it requires a **small language model** that can efficiently handle translations in real-time without draining device resources or impacting performance.

The solution needs to balance the size and speed of the model while maintaining an acceptable level of translation accuracy. The company decides to implement a **small transformer-based language model** like distilBART or MarianMT, fine-tuned specifically for translation tasks, and deploy it to mobile devices.

Solution Approach:

We will leverage Hugging Face's MarianMT, a multilingual transformer model pre-trained for machine translation tasks, which is smaller than many other models used for this task. MarianMT is designed to handle multiple languages and is optimized for efficient translation, making it ideal for real-time use on smartphones.

Steps:

1. **Dataset Collection**: Collect bilingual text datasets for training the translation model (e.g., English-to-Spanish, French-to-English).
2. **Model Selection**: Choose a pre-trained MarianMT model that supports multilingual translation and is optimized for smaller sizes.
3. **Fine-Tuning**: Fine-tune the MarianMT model using the collected dataset to improve performance on the specific translation task.
4. **Deployment**: Deploy the fine-tuned model on mobile devices using efficient libraries like TensorFlow Lite or ONNX for better performance on resource-constrained devices.

Implementation Details

We will use the Hugging Face transformers library to load the pre-trained MarianMT model and fine-tune it for a specific language pair. Then, we'll integrate the model into a mobile-friendly format for deployment.

1. Installing Required Libraries

First, install the required libraries using pip:

pip install transformers datasets torch

2. Data Preprocessing

We'll use a sample multilingual dataset to fine-tune the

translation model. For this case, we'll use English-to-Spanish translation.

```
from datasets import load_dataset
from transformers import MarianMTModel, MarianTokenizer

# Load the bilingual English-Spanish dataset
dataset = load_dataset("wmt16", "ro-en")

# Load pre-trained MarianMT tokenizer
tokenizer = MarianTokenizer.from_pretrained('Helsinki-NLP/opus-mt-en-es')

# Function to tokenize the dataset
def tokenize_function(examples):
    return tokenizer(examples['en'], padding="max_length", truncation=True)

# Tokenize the training and testing datasets
tokenized_datasets = dataset.map(tokenize_function, batched=True)
```

3. Fine-tuning the MarianMT Model

Now, we'll load the pre-trained MarianMT model and fine-tune it on our dataset for English-to-Spanish translation.

```
from transformers import Trainer, TrainingArguments

# Load the pre-trained MarianMT model for translation
model = MarianMTModel.from_pretrained('Helsinki-NLP/opus-mt-en-es')

# Set up the training arguments
```

```
training_args = TrainingArguments(
    output_dir='./results',         # Output directory
    evaluation_strategy="epoch",    # Evaluate after every epoch
    learning_rate=2e-5,             # Learning rate
    per_device_train_batch_size=16, # Batch size per device during training
    per_device_eval_batch_size=16,  # Batch size per device during evaluation
    num_train_epochs=3,             # Number of training epochs
    weight_decay=0.01,              # Strength of weight decay
)

# Initialize Trainer
trainer = Trainer(
    model=model,                    # The model to train
    args=training_args,             # The training arguments
    train_dataset=tokenized_datasets['train'],  # The training dataset
    eval_dataset=tokenized_datasets['test']     # The evaluation dataset
)

# Train the model
trainer.train()
```

4. Model Evaluation

After fine-tuning, evaluate the model's performance on the test dataset to check its translation accuracy.

```
# Evaluate the model
results = trainer.evaluate()
```

```
# Print the evaluation results
print(f"Test Results: {results}")
```

5. Translating New Text

Once the model is fine-tuned, you can use it for real-time translation of new sentences.

```
# Function to translate text from English to Spanish
def translate_text(input_text):
    inputs = tokenizer(input_text, return_tensors="pt", padding=True, truncation=True, max_length=512)
    translated = model.generate(inputs)
    translation = tokenizer.decode(translated[0], skip_special_tokens=True)
    return translation

# Example of translation
input_text = "Hello, how are you?"
print("Original Text:", input_text)
print("Translated Text:", translate_text(input_text))
```

6. Deployment for Mobile Devices

Once the model is fine-tuned, you can deploy it on a mobile device using frameworks like **TensorFlow Lite** or **ONNX** for efficient inference on smartphones.

For example, converting the model to TensorFlow Lite:

```
# Install TensorFlow and TensorFlow Lite converter
pip install tensorflow

# Convert the PyTorch model to TensorFlow
import tensorflow as tf
```

```
from transformers import TFAutoModelForSeq2SeqLM

# Load the fine-tuned model
tf_model = TFAutoModelForSeq2SeqLM.from_pretrained('path_to_finetuned_model')

# Convert to TensorFlow Lite format
converter = tf.lite.TFLiteConverter.from_keras_model(tf_model)
tflite_model = converter.convert()

# Save the converted model
with open('model.tflite', 'wb') as f:
    f.write(tflite_model)
```

This will allow the model to be deployed efficiently on mobile devices while maintaining low latency for real-time translation.

Key Results and Impact

- **Real-Time Translation**: The fine-tuned MarianMT model offers real-time translation between languages, making it an excellent tool for travelers who need quick translations on the go.
- **Resource Efficiency**: By using a small, fine-tuned model like MarianMT, the app performs well on resource-constrained devices, ensuring that it doesn't compromise the smartphone's performance.
- **Scalability**: The model can be extended to support multiple languages by fine-tuning on additional datasets for other language pairs (e.g., Spanish-to-English, French-to-English).

- **Global Accessibility**: The compact model ensures that users in emerging economies with limited access to high-performance devices can still benefit from advanced translation capabilities.

Conclusion

This case study highlights how **compact AI** can be effectively deployed in **real-time machine translation** applications, such as mobile translation apps. By using a smaller, optimized model like **MarianMT**, developers can provide users with fast, reliable, and resource-efficient language translation on smartphones, helping overcome language barriers for travelers around the world.

CASE STUDY: COMPACT AI FOR DOCUMENT PROCESSING AND AUTOMATED DATA EXTRACTION IN LEGAL DOCUMENTS

Background:

A legal firm needs an efficient way to process large volumes of legal documents, including contracts, agreements, and court orders. These documents contain complex legal jargon, and manually extracting data such as terms, conditions, clauses, dates, parties involved, and legal precedents is time-consuming and prone to human error. The firm wants to automate this process using **compact AI models** that can quickly and accurately process documents and extract meaningful data.

The goal is to build a **compact AI-based document processing system** that can read, understand, and extract data from legal documents in near real-time with minimal resource requirements. The solution needs to operate efficiently on limited hardware like document scanners and low-power desktop systems.

Solution Approach:

The firm decides to implement a **small NLP model** for **document processing** using techniques like **named entity recognition (NER)**, **text classification**, and **extraction of key information**. For this purpose, we can utilize **DistilBERT**, a smaller version of BERT (Bidirectional Encoder Representations from Transformers), optimized for processing tasks with less computational power.

Steps:

1. **Dataset Collection**: Collect legal documents (e.g., contracts, court orders, terms and conditions) for training and testing.
2. **Preprocessing**: Annotate a set of documents with metadata (e.g., names, dates, legal terms) to create training data.
3. **Model Selection and Training**: Fine-tune a small transformer-based NLP model like **DistilBERT** using the annotated data.
4. **Deployment**: Deploy the trained model for document processing using optimized libraries like TensorFlow, ONNX, or TensorFlow Lite.

Implementation Details

1. Installing Required Libraries

First, install the required libraries using pip:

```
pip install transformers datasets torch
```

2. Data Preprocessing

For this case, we'll simulate data preprocessing from annotated legal documents.

```
from datasets import load_dataset
```

```
from transformers import
DistilBertTokenizer, DistilBertForTokenClassification, Trainer,
TrainingArguments
import torch

# Sample annotated legal dataset for training
legal_documents = [
    {"text": "Contract between ABC Corp and XYZ Ltd. dated
March 2023. Terms include confidentiality and payment
terms.", "entities": [(0, 3, "Company"), (10, 13, "Company"), (23,
24, "Date"), (32, 45, "Legal Term")]},
    {"text": "Court order dated April 2023 mandates compliance
to anti-bribery clauses between John Doe and the state.",
"entities": [(0, 4, "Person"), (18, 21, "State"), (23, 28, "Date"), (32,
42, "Legal Term")]}
]

# Tokenizer for DistilBERT
tokenizer = DistilBertTokenizer.from_pretrained('distilbert-
base-uncased')

# Function to tokenize documents
def tokenize_and_align_labels(examples):
    tokenized_inputs = tokenizer(examples['text'],
truncation=True, padding='max_length', max_length=128)
    labels = [{"entity": entity[2], "start": entity[0], "end":
entity[1]} for entity in examples['entities']]
    tokenized_inputs['labels'] = labels
    return tokenized_inputs

# Preprocess the dataset
```

```
tokenized_dataset = list(map(tokenize_and_align_labels, legal_documents))
```

3. Model Training

Now, fine-tune the DistilBERT model using tokenized documents.

```
from transformers import TrainingArguments, Trainer, DistilBertForTokenClassification

# Define the training arguments
training_args = TrainingArguments(
    output_dir='./results',          # Output directory for model checkpoints
    learning_rate=2e-5,
    num_train_epochs=3,
    per_device_train_batch_size=16,
    weight_decay=0.01,
    evaluation_strategy="epoch",
)

# Load the DistilBERT model
model = DistilBertForTokenClassification.from_pretrained('distilbert-base-uncased', num_labels=len(set([entity[2] for entity in legal_documents])))

# Define the trainer
trainer = Trainer(
    model=model,
    args=training_args,
```

```
    train_dataset=tokenized_dataset
)

# Train the model
trainer.train()
```

4. Model Evaluation

After fine-tuning, evaluate the model's performance:

```
# Evaluate the trained model
trainer.evaluate()
```

5. Document Processing with Compact AI

Once the model is fine-tuned, use it to process new documents in near real-time:

```
# Function to process new documents
def process_document(document, model, tokenizer):
    inputs = tokenizer(document, return_tensors="pt", padding='max_length', truncation=True, max_length=128)
    outputs = model(inputs)
    predicted_entities = [(tokenizer.decode(idx), entity['entity']) for idx, entity in zip(inputs['input_ids'][0], outputs.logits[0])]
    return predicted_entities

# Example of document processing
document = "Contract between ABC Corp and XYZ Ltd. dated March 2023. Terms include confidentiality and payment terms."
print("Document:", document)
print("Processed Entities:", process_document(document, model, tokenizer))
```

6. Deployment

For deployment, use optimized models like **TensorFlow Lite** or **ONNX** to run the model efficiently on resource-constrained devices (e.g., document scanners, low-power desktop systems).

```
# Install TensorFlow and TensorFlow Lite converter
pip install tensorflow

# Convert the trained model to TensorFlow format
import tensorflow as tf

# Convert from Hugging Face's model to TensorFlow format
tf_model = tf.saved_model.load('path_to_finetuned_model')

# Save the model in TensorFlow Lite format
converter = tf.lite.TFLiteConverter.from_saved_model('path_to_finetuned_model')
tflite_model = converter.convert()

# Save the converted model
with open('document_processor.tflite', 'wb') as f:
    f.write(tflite_model)
```

Key Results and Impact

- **Document Processing Efficiency**: The compact AI-based document processing system successfully extracts relevant information from legal documents with high accuracy (e.g., entity recognition like "Company", "Date", "Person", "Legal Term").
- **Resource Efficiency**: By deploying a smaller transformer-based model like **DistilBERT**, document processing can be performed efficiently on low-

power hardware like document scanners and low-power desktop systems.

- **Scalability**: The system can handle multiple legal document types and adapt to various languages and legal systems with minimal adjustments.
- **Accessibility**: Legal firms in emerging markets with less access to high-performance computing resources can still leverage automated document processing solutions.

Conclusion

This case study demonstrates the use of compact AI models like **DistilBERT** for document processing and automated data extraction in legal documents. By using a smaller, optimized model for document analysis, legal firms can significantly reduce costs, improve processing accuracy, and increase accessibility to automated solutions for data extraction.

CASE STUDY: REAL-TIME SENTIMENT ANALYSIS FOR SOCIAL MEDIA MONITORING WITH COMPACT AI MODELS

Background:

A leading digital marketing agency specializes in social media monitoring for brands across multiple industries. The agency's goal is to quickly analyze customer sentiments from social media platforms such as Twitter, Facebook, and Instagram to track brand perception and customer feedback.

With the increasing volume of social media posts, the agency needed an **efficient sentiment analysis system** that could process vast amounts of unstructured text data in real-time. However, due to resource constraints and the need for faster processing, the agency opted to use **small language models** instead of large transformer models like BERT or GPT.

They selected a **DistilBERT** model to perform sentiment analysis due to its smaller size, faster processing time, and competitive performance. By using a **lightweight model**, the agency could deploy it across multiple social media platforms for real-time sentiment tracking.

Solution Approach:

1. **Data Collection**: The agency gathered data from various social media platforms using public APIs, including customer comments, reviews, and tweets related to their clients' brands.
2. **Model Selection**: A **DistilBERT** model pre-trained on general language tasks was fine-tuned for sentiment analysis using the collected social media data.
3. **Model Fine-Tuning**: The agency fine-tuned the model using labeled data (positive, neutral, and negative sentiment) to classify the sentiment of social media posts.
4. **Deployment**: The sentiment analysis model was deployed as an API service to monitor and analyze incoming social media content in real-time.

Implementation Details

1. Install Required Libraries

```
pip install transformers torch Flask
```

2. Data Preparation

The agency prepared a dataset consisting of social media posts labeled with sentiment categories (positive, neutral, negative).

```
import pandas as pd

# Example social media post data with sentiment labels
data = {
    'post': [
        'I love the new product! It works great!',
        'The service was okay, nothing special.',
        'I hate how slow their customer support is.'
```

```
    ],
    'sentiment': ['positive', 'neutral', 'negative']
}

df = pd.DataFrame(data)
```

3. Tokenization and Model Setup

The team loads the **DistilBERT** model and tokenizer for fine-tuning.

```
from transformers import DistilBertTokenizer, DistilBertForSequenceClassification
from torch.utils.data import DataLoader, TensorDataset
import torch

# Load the DistilBERT tokenizer and model
tokenizer = DistilBertTokenizer.from_pretrained('distilbert-base-uncased')
model = DistilBertForSequenceClassification.from_pretrained('distilbert-base-uncased', num_labels=3)

# Tokenize the posts
inputs = tokenizer(df['post'].tolist(), padding=True, truncation=True, return_tensors='pt', max_length=50)

# Map sentiment labels to integers
label_mapping = {'positive': 0, 'neutral': 1, 'negative': 2}
labels = [label_mapping[sentiment] for sentiment in df['sentiment']]

# Convert labels to tensor
```

```
labels_tensor = torch.tensor(labels)

# Create TensorDataset
dataset = TensorDataset(inputs['input_ids'], inputs['attention_mask'], labels_tensor)

# Create DataLoader for training
train_dataloader = DataLoader(dataset, batch_size=2, shuffle=True)
```

4. Model Fine-Tuning

The team fine-tunes the **DistilBERT** model on the sentiment-labeled dataset.

```
from transformers import AdamW
from torch.optim import Adam

# Define optimizer and loss function
optimizer = AdamW(model.parameters(), lr=1e-5)

# Fine-tune the model
model.train()
for epoch in range(3):
    for batch in train_dataloader:
        input_ids, attention_mask, labels = batch
        optimizer.zero_grad()

        # Forward pass
        outputs = model(input_ids, attention_mask=attention_mask, labels=labels)
        loss = outputs.loss
```

```
        # Backward pass
        loss.backward()
        optimizer.step()

    print(f"Epoch {epoch+1}: Loss = {loss.item()}")
```

5. Deploying the Sentiment Analysis API with Flask

After fine-tuning, the sentiment analysis model is deployed via a Flask application to provide real-time sentiment analysis for new social media posts.

```
from flask import Flask, request, jsonify

# Initialize Flask app
app = Flask(__name__)

# Set the model to evaluation mode
model.eval()

@app.route('/sentiment', methods=['POST'])
def sentiment_analysis():
    user_post = request.json['post']

    # Tokenize the user post
    inputs = tokenizer(user_post, return_tensors='pt', padding=True, truncation=True, max_length=50)

    with torch.no_grad():
        outputs = model(inputs)
        logits = outputs.logits
```

```
    # Get the predicted sentiment label
    predicted_class = torch.argmax(logits, dim=1).item()
    sentiment_label = {0: 'positive', 1: 'neutral', 2: 'negative'}
[predicted_class]

    return jsonify({"sentiment": sentiment_label})

if __name__ == "__main__":
    app.run(debug=True)
```

6. Testing the API

To test the API, you can send a POST request with a social media post and get the sentiment label.

```
import requests

# Test the sentiment analysis service
url = "http://127.0.0.1:5000/sentiment"
data = {
    "post": "I absolutely love this product!"
}

response = requests.post(url, json=data)
print(response.json())
```

The response might look like:

```
{
    "sentiment": "positive"
}
```

Key Results and Impact

- **Real-Time Sentiment Monitoring**: The sentiment

analysis system allows the agency to track brand perception on social media in real time. Positive, negative, and neutral sentiments are automatically classified and monitored.

- **Scalability**: By using a **DistilBERT**-based compact model, the agency can scale the solution to handle large volumes of social media posts without the need for heavy computational resources.
- **Cost-Effective**: **Small language models** like **DistilBERT** reduce operational costs by requiring less infrastructure and providing faster processing speeds.
- **Improved Brand Strategy**: The agency can now provide immediate insights to clients about public sentiment, enabling brands to adjust their marketing and customer support strategies promptly.

Conclusion

This case study showcases the potential of **small language models** for **real-time sentiment analysis** in high-volume social media monitoring. By using a **DistilBERT** model, the agency was able to provide an efficient and cost-effective solution that allowed them to track customer sentiment across global social platforms. The model's lightweight nature ensured **quick analysis** without sacrificing performance, demonstrating the viability of compact AI models for scalable, real-time applications in customer experience and digital marketing.

CASE STUDY: REAL-TIME LANGUAGE TRANSLATION WITH COMPACT AI MODELS FOR GLOBAL CUSTOMER SUPPORT

Background:

A multinational e-commerce company with customers across the globe wanted to offer **real-time language translation** for customer support. They aimed to provide seamless communication between their customers and support agents, regardless of the customer's native language. To achieve this, the company decided to implement a **real-time translation chatbot** that would translate queries in multiple languages and offer responses in the user's preferred language.

Given the budget constraints and the need for a fast, lightweight solution, they chose to implement a **small language model** for their translation engine, particularly focusing on multilingual support. The team decided to use a **compact BERT-based multilingual model**, such as **DistilBERT**, fine-tuned for language translation tasks.

Solution Approach:

1. **Data Collection**: The company collected a multilingual dataset of customer support queries and responses across multiple languages, including English, Spanish, French, and Mandarin.
2. **Model Selection**: The team opted for a **DistilBERT**-based model, which is smaller and faster than traditional transformer-based models like the original BERT but still offers competitive performance for translation tasks.
3. **Model Fine-Tuning**: The team fine-tuned the model on their multilingual dataset to specialize in translating queries into the desired languages.
4. **Deployment**: The translation model was deployed as a backend service, enabling seamless real-time translation in the e-commerce website's chat feature.

Implementation Details

1. Install Required Libraries

```
pip install transformers torch Flask
```

2. Data Preparation

The company prepared a multilingual dataset of customer queries and responses.

```
import pandas as pd

# Sample multilingual customer query and response data
data = {
    'query': [
        'How do I track my order?',
        '¿Cómo puedo rastrear mi pedido?',
        'Comment puis-je suivre ma commande?',
        '如何跟踪我的订单？'
```

```
    ],
    'response': [
        'You can track your order by visiting the "Order Status" page in your account.',
        'Puedes rastrear tu pedido visitando la página "Estado de mi pedido" en tu cuenta.',
        'Vous pouvez suivre votre commande en visitant la page "Suivi de ma commande" dans votre compte.',
        '您可以访问“我的订单状态”页面来跟踪您的订单。'
    ]
}

df = pd.DataFrame(data)
```

3. Tokenization and Model Preparation

We load the **DistilBERT** multilingual model and tokenizer. The dataset is tokenized for fine-tuning.

```
from transformers import DistilBertTokenizer, DistilBertForSequenceClassification, Trainer, TrainingArguments
import torch

# Load the tokenizer and model
tokenizer = DistilBertTokenizer.from_pretrained('distilbert-base-multilingual-cased')
model = DistilBertForSequenceClassification.from_pretrained('distilbert-base-multilingual-cased')

# Tokenize the data
inputs = tokenizer(df['query'].tolist(), padding=True,
```

```
truncation=True, return_tensors='pt', max_length=50)
labels = tokenizer(df['response'].tolist(), padding=True, truncation=True, return_tensors='pt', max_length=100).input_ids
labels = torch.tensor(labels)

# Prepare dataset
dataset = torch.utils.data.TensorDataset(inputs['input_ids'], labels)
```

4. Fine-Tuning the Model

We fine-tune the **DistilBERT** multilingual model on the customer support queries and responses.

```
# Set up training arguments
training_args = TrainingArguments(
    output_dir='./results',          # output directory
    num_train_epochs=3,              # number of training epochs
    per_device_train_batch_size=2,  # batch size for training
    logging_dir='./logs',            # directory for storing logs
    logging_steps=100,
)

# Initialize Trainer
trainer = Trainer(
    model=model,
    args=training_args,
    train_dataset=dataset,
)

# Fine-tune the model
```

trainer.train()

5. Deploying the Translation Service with Flask

After fine-tuning, we deploy the translation model using Flask for real-time interaction. The system receives a query in any supported language, translates it to the desired language, and returns the response.

```
from flask import Flask, request, jsonify

# Initialize Flask app
app = Flask(__name__)

# Set the model to evaluation mode
model.eval()

@app.route('/translate', methods=['POST'])
def translate():
    user_message = request.json['message']
    target_language = request.json.get('target_language', 'en') #
Default to English

    # Tokenize the user message
    inputs = tokenizer.encode(user_message,
return_tensors='pt')

    # Translate the message
    with torch.no_grad():
        outputs = model.generate(inputs, max_length=50,
num_return_sequences=1)

    # Decode the output tokens
```

```
    translated_message = tokenizer.decode(outputs[0], skip_special_tokens=True)

    # Translate to the target language (for simplicity, we'll assume that it's mapped directly)
    # In real-world cases, we could use external translation services or more advanced handling
    translated_response = f"Translation to {target_language}: {translated_message}"

    return jsonify({"response": translated_response})

if __name__ == "__main__":
    app.run(debug=True)
```

6. Testing the Translation Service

We can now test the translation chatbot by sending a POST request with a query and target language.

```
import requests

# Test the translation service
url = "http://127.0.0.1:5000/translate"
data = {
    "message": "How do I track my order?",
    "target_language": "es"  # Spanish
}

response = requests.post(url, json=data)
print(response.json())
```

The response might look like this:

```
{
```

"response": "Translation to es: Puedes rastrear tu pedido visitando la página 'Estado de mi pedido' en tu cuenta."

}

Key Results and Impact

- **Multilingual Support**: The chatbot can now support customers in multiple languages, enhancing the global reach of the company.
- **Real-Time Translation**: The **DistilBERT** model enables real-time translation of customer queries and responses, providing an interactive and engaging experience.
- **Compact Model Efficiency**: The **small size of DistilBERT** made it possible to deploy the translation system efficiently on edge devices, ensuring low latency and minimal computational resources.
- **Cost-Effective**: The use of a **small language model** reduced the infrastructure and operational costs compared to traditional translation systems that require large models and high computational power.
- **Improved Customer Experience**: By providing quick, accurate, and language-appropriate responses, the company significantly improved customer satisfaction and engagement.

Conclusion

This case study illustrates the power of **small language models** for **real-time multilingual translation**, particularly in a customer support context. The use of a **compact, fine-tuned model like DistilBERT** allowed the company to achieve a balance between **speed**, **performance**, and **resource-efficiency**, enabling them to offer real-time support to a global customer base. The solution reduced costs while improving user experience, demonstrating the potential of **compact AI** to scale across industries and geographies.

Case Study: Efficient Chatbot Development with Small Language Models for Customer Support

Background:

A telecommunications company wanted to build a **customer support chatbot** to handle common customer queries and reduce the load on their support team. The chatbot needed to be efficient, capable of answering questions regarding billing, plan changes, and service issues. Given the growing number of customers, they required a solution that could scale without requiring significant computational resources.

To achieve this, the company decided to implement a **small language model** for the chatbot's Natural Language Understanding (NLU) component. They chose to use **DistilGPT-2**, a lightweight version of the GPT-2 model, because of its good performance in conversational tasks and its smaller size compared to the original GPT-2.

Solution Approach:

1. **Data Collection**: The company collected historical customer support interactions, focusing on FAQs related to billing, service plans, and technical issues.
2. **Model Selection**: The team selected **DistilGPT-2** due to its lightweight architecture that provides an excellent balance between speed and performance for text generation tasks.
3. **Model Fine-Tuning**: They fine-tuned the model on the collected data to specialize in customer support conversations.
4. **Deployment**: The chatbot was deployed on the company's website and mobile app, enabling customers to receive immediate responses to common questions.

Implementation Details

1. Install Required Libraries

```
pip install transformers torch Flask
```

2. Data Preparation

The company prepared a dataset containing common customer queries and responses.

```
import pandas as pd

# Sample customer query and response data
data = {
    'query': [
        'How can I change my billing address?',
        'What are the available service plans?',
        'My internet is not working, what should I do?',
        'How can I upgrade my plan?',
        'What is my current balance?'
    ],
    'response': [
        'To change your billing address, log in to your account and update your personal information under the Billing section.',
        'We offer several service plans, including Basic, Premium, and Ultimate. You can find detailed comparisons on our website.',
        'Try restarting your modem. If the issue persists, please contact our technical support team.',
        'You can upgrade your plan by visiting the Plans section in your account settings.',
        'You can view your balance by logging into your account
```

```
and checking your account dashboard.'
    ]
}

df = pd.DataFrame(data)
```

3. Tokenization and Model Preparation

We load **DistilGPT-2** and prepare the dataset for fine-tuning. The queries will serve as input, and the responses will be the target output.

```
from transformers import GPT2Tokenizer, GPT2LMHeadModel, Trainer, TrainingArguments
import torch

# Load the tokenizer and model
tokenizer = GPT2Tokenizer.from_pretrained('distilgpt2')
model = GPT2LMHeadModel.from_pretrained('distilgpt2')

# Tokenize the data
inputs = tokenizer(df['query'].tolist(), padding=True, truncation=True, return_tensors='pt', max_length=50)
labels = tokenizer(df['response'].tolist(), padding=True, truncation=True, return_tensors='pt', max_length=100).input_ids
labels = torch.tensor(labels)

# Adjust labels: GPT2 expects the labels to be shifted by one token
labels = labels[:, 1:].contiguous()

# Prepare dataset
```

dataset = torch.utils.data.TensorDataset(inputs['input_ids'], labels)

4. Fine-Tuning the Model

We fine-tune the **DistilGPT-2** model on the customer support queries and responses.

```
# Set up training arguments
training_args = TrainingArguments(
    output_dir='./results',          # output directory
    num_train_epochs=3,              # number of training epochs
    per_device_train_batch_size=2,   # batch size for training
    logging_dir='./logs',            # directory for storing logs
    logging_steps=100,
)

# Initialize Trainer
trainer = Trainer(
    model=model,
    args=training_args,
    train_dataset=dataset,
)

# Fine-tune the model
trainer.train()
```

5. Deploying the Chatbot with Flask

After fine-tuning, we deploy the chatbot using Flask for real-time interaction.

```
from flask import Flask, request, jsonify
```

```
# Initialize Flask app
app = Flask(__name__)

# Set the model to evaluation mode
model.eval()

@app.route('/chat', methods=['POST'])
def chat():
    user_message = request.json['message']

    # Tokenize the user message
    inputs = tokenizer.encode(user_message,
return_tensors='pt')

    # Generate a response from the model
    with torch.no_grad():
        outputs = model.generate(inputs, max_length=50,
num_return_sequences=1)

    # Decode the output tokens
    chatbot_response = tokenizer.decode(outputs[0],
skip_special_tokens=True)

    return jsonify({"response": chatbot_response})

if __name__ == "__main__":
    app.run(debug=True)
```

6. Testing the Chatbot

We can now test the chatbot by sending a POST request with a query.

```
import requests

# Test the chatbot
url = "http://127.0.0.1:5000/chat"
data = {"message": "How can I change my billing address?"}

response = requests.post(url, json=data)
print(response.json())
```

The response might look like this:

```
{
    "response": "To change your billing address, log in to your account and update your personal information under the Billing section."
}
```

Key Results and Impact

- **Real-Time Support**: The chatbot could answer common customer queries in real-time, reducing wait times for customers and offloading the burden from human agents.
- **Compact and Efficient**: **DistilGPT-2** offered a great balance between model performance and size, ensuring fast response times and reducing the computational resources required for deployment.
- **Scalability**: The chatbot could easily scale to handle thousands of queries daily without major infrastructure changes, making it ideal for growing businesses.
- **Improved Customer Satisfaction**: By providing instant responses to common issues, customers received faster resolutions, improving their overall

satisfaction.

- **Cost-Effective**: The small model allowed the company to deploy the solution on low-cost cloud services, keeping operational costs low compared to deploying larger models.

Conclusion

This case study demonstrates how **small language models** like **DistilGPT-2** can be effectively utilized to create a **cost-effective and scalable chatbot** for customer support. The small model allowed the company to provide real-time, accurate responses to customer inquiries, thereby improving operational efficiency and customer satisfaction. It also highlighted how **compact AI** can offer significant benefits in terms of performance, scalability, and cost, making it a practical solution for customer service automation.

Case Study: Efficient Chatbot Development with Small Language Models for Customer Support

Background:

A telecommunications company wanted to build a **customer support chatbot** to handle common customer queries and reduce the load on their support team. The chatbot needed to be efficient, capable of answering questions regarding billing, plan changes, and service issues. Given the growing number of customers, they required a solution that could scale without requiring significant computational resources.

To achieve this, the company decided to implement a **small language model** for the chatbot's Natural Language Understanding (NLU) component. They chose to use **DistilGPT-2**, a lightweight version of the GPT-2 model, because of its good performance in conversational tasks and its smaller size compared to the original GPT-2.

Solution Approach:

1. **Data Collection**: The company collected historical customer support interactions, focusing on FAQs related to billing, service plans, and technical issues.
2. **Model Selection**: The team selected **DistilGPT-2** due to its lightweight architecture that provides an excellent balance between speed and performance for text generation tasks.
3. **Model Fine-Tuning**: They fine-tuned the model on the collected data to specialize in customer support conversations.
4. **Deployment**: The chatbot was deployed on the company's website and mobile app, enabling customers to receive immediate responses to common questions.

Implementation Details

1. Install Required Libraries

```
pip install transformers torch Flask
```

2. Data Preparation

The company prepared a dataset containing common customer queries and responses.

```
import pandas as pd

# Sample customer query and response data
data = {
    'query': [
        'How can I change my billing address?',
        'What are the available service plans?',
        'My internet is not working, what should I do?',
        'How can I upgrade my plan?',
        'What is my current balance?'
```

```
    ],
    'response': [
        'To change your billing address, log in to your account and update your personal information under the Billing section.',
        'We offer several service plans, including Basic, Premium, and Ultimate. You can find detailed comparisons on our website.',
        'Try restarting your modem. If the issue persists, please contact our technical support team.',
        'You can upgrade your plan by visiting the Plans section in your account settings.',
        'You can view your balance by logging into your account and checking your account dashboard.'
    ]
}

df = pd.DataFrame(data)
```

3. Tokenization and Model Preparation

We load **DistilGPT-2** and prepare the dataset for fine-tuning. The queries will serve as input, and the responses will be the target output.

```
from transformers import GPT2Tokenizer, GPT2LMHeadModel, Trainer, TrainingArguments
import torch

# Load the tokenizer and model
tokenizer = GPT2Tokenizer.from_pretrained('distilgpt2')
model = GPT2LMHeadModel.from_pretrained('distilgpt2')
```

```
# Tokenize the data
inputs = tokenizer(df['query'].tolist(), padding=True, truncation=True, return_tensors='pt', max_length=50)
labels = tokenizer(df['response'].tolist(), padding=True, truncation=True, return_tensors='pt', max_length=100).input_ids
labels = torch.tensor(labels)

# Adjust labels: GPT2 expects the labels to be shifted by one token
labels = labels[:, 1:].contiguous()

# Prepare dataset
dataset = torch.utils.data.TensorDataset(inputs['input_ids'], labels)
```

4. Fine-Tuning the Model

We fine-tune the **DistilGPT-2** model on the customer support queries and responses.

```
# Set up training arguments
training_args = TrainingArguments(
    output_dir='./results',          # output directory
    num_train_epochs=3,              # number of training epochs
    per_device_train_batch_size=2,   # batch size for training
    logging_dir='./logs',            # directory for storing logs
    logging_steps=100,
)

# Initialize Trainer
```

```
trainer = Trainer(
    model=model,
    args=training_args,
    train_dataset=dataset,
)

# Fine-tune the model
trainer.train()
```

5. Deploying the Chatbot with Flask

After fine-tuning, we deploy the chatbot using Flask for real-time interaction.

```
from flask import Flask, request, jsonify

# Initialize Flask app
app = Flask(__name__)

# Set the model to evaluation mode
model.eval()

@app.route('/chat', methods=['POST'])
def chat():
    user_message = request.json['message']

    # Tokenize the user message
    inputs = tokenizer.encode(user_message, return_tensors='pt')

    # Generate a response from the model
    with torch.no_grad():
```

```
    outputs = model.generate(inputs, max_length=50, num_return_sequences=1)

    # Decode the output tokens
    chatbot_response = tokenizer.decode(outputs[0], skip_special_tokens=True)

    return jsonify({"response": chatbot_response})

if __name__ == "__main__":
    app.run(debug=True)
```

6. Testing the Chatbot

We can now test the chatbot by sending a POST request with a query.

```
import requests

# Test the chatbot
url = "http://127.0.0.1:5000/chat"
data = {"message": "How can I change my billing address?"}

response = requests.post(url, json=data)
print(response.json())
```

The response might look like this:

```
{
    "response": "To change your billing address, log in to your account and update your personal information under the Billing section."
}
```

Key Results and Impact

- **Real-Time Support**: The chatbot could answer

common customer queries in real-time, reducing wait times for customers and offloading the burden from human agents.

- **Compact and Efficient**: **DistilGPT-2** offered a great balance between model performance and size, ensuring fast response times and reducing the computational resources required for deployment.
- **Scalability**: The chatbot could easily scale to handle thousands of queries daily without major infrastructure changes, making it ideal for growing businesses.
- **Improved Customer Satisfaction**: By providing instant responses to common issues, customers received faster resolutions, improving their overall satisfaction.
- **Cost-Effective**: The small model allowed the company to deploy the solution on low-cost cloud services, keeping operational costs low compared to deploying larger models.

Conclusion

This case study demonstrates how **small language models** like **DistilGPT-2** can be effectively utilized to create a **cost-effective and scalable chatbot** for customer support. The small model allowed the company to provide real-time, accurate responses to customer inquiries, thereby improving operational efficiency and customer satisfaction. It also highlighted how **compact AI** can offer significant benefits in terms of performance, scalability, and cost, making it a practical solution for customer service automation.

Case Study: Real-Time Customer Sentiment Analysis for E-Commerce Using Compact AI Models

Background:

A rapidly growing e-commerce company wanted to enhance its customer experience by analyzing customer sentiment from product reviews. The goal was to understand how customers felt about various products, identify any potential issues, and respond quickly to negative sentiments. However, the company needed a solution that could run in real-time on a budget-friendly cloud platform. They decided to use **small language models** for this task to balance performance with efficiency.

The team chose to fine-tune a **DistilBERT** model for **sentiment analysis**. DistilBERT, being a smaller version of BERT, is ideal for deploying on cloud platforms with resource constraints while still providing competitive accuracy for NLP tasks.

Solution Approach:

1. **Data Collection**: The company collected a dataset of customer reviews, including ratings (positive/negative) and review text.
2. **Model Selection**: The team selected **DistilBERT** due to its smaller size and ability to perform well on text classification tasks like sentiment analysis.
3. **Model Training**: They fine-tuned DistilBERT on the sentiment-labeled dataset of product reviews.
4. **Real-Time Application**: The model was deployed via an API, allowing the company to analyze customer sentiment in real-time as new reviews were posted.

Implementation Details

1. Install Required Libraries

pip install transformers torch scikit-learn Flask pandas

2. Data Preparation

The dataset consists of customer reviews, each labeled as either "positive" or "negative".

```
import pandas as pd

# Sample dataset of customer reviews and their sentiment labels
data = {
    'review': [
        'This product is fantastic, I love it!',
        'Terrible quality, will never buy again.',
        'Good value for money, highly recommend.',
        'The worst purchase I made, complete waste of money.',
        'Very satisfied with the product, it works great.'
    ],
    'sentiment': [1, 0, 1, 0, 1] # 1 = positive, 0 = negative
}

df = pd.DataFrame(data)
```

3. Tokenization and Model Preparation

We tokenize the review text and prepare the model for training.

```
from transformers import DistilBertTokenizer
import torch

# Load the DistilBERT tokenizer
tokenizer = DistilBertTokenizer.from_pretrained('distilbert-base-uncased')

# Tokenize the reviews
inputs = tokenizer(df['review'].tolist(), padding=True, truncation=True, return_tensors='pt')
```

labels = torch.tensor(df['sentiment'].tolist())

4. Model Setup and Fine-Tuning

We fine-tune the **DistilBERT** model for sentiment classification.

```
from transformers import DistilBertForSequenceClassification, Trainer, TrainingArguments

# Load DistilBERT for binary classification (positive/negative sentiment)
model = DistilBertForSequenceClassification.from_pretrained('distilbert-base-uncased', num_labels=2)

# Set up training arguments
training_args = TrainingArguments(
    output_dir='./results',          # output directory
    num_train_epochs=3,              # number of training epochs
    per_device_train_batch_size=8,   # batch size for training
    logging_dir='./logs',            # directory for storing logs
)

# Initialize Trainer
trainer = Trainer(
    model=model,
    args=training_args,
    train_dataset=torch.utils.data.TensorDataset(inputs['input_ids'], labels),
)
```

```
# Fine-tune the model
trainer.train()
```

5. Deploy the Sentiment Analysis API Using Flask

Once the model is fine-tuned, we create an API that can analyze customer sentiment in real time.

```
from flask import Flask, request, jsonify

# Initialize Flask app
app = Flask(__name__)

# Load the fine-tuned model
model.eval()

@app.route('/sentiment-analysis', methods=['POST'])
def sentiment_analysis():
    # Get the review from the POST request
    review_data = request.json
    review_text = review_data['review']

    # Tokenize the review text
    inputs = tokenizer(review_text, return_tensors='pt',
padding=True, truncation=True)

    # Get the model's prediction
    with torch.no_grad():
        outputs = model(inputs)
        predicted_class = torch.argmax(outputs.logits,
dim=1).item()
```

```
    # Map the predicted class to the corresponding label
    sentiment = 'Positive' if predicted_class == 1 else 'Negative'

    return jsonify({"sentiment": sentiment})

if __name__ == "__main__":
    app.run(debug=True)
```

6. Testing the Sentiment Analysis API

You can now test the sentiment analysis API by sending a POST request with a customer review.

```
import requests

# Send a customer review to the sentiment analysis API
url = "http://127.0.0.1:5000/sentiment-analysis"
review = {"review": "This product is amazing, will buy again!"}

response = requests.post(url, json=review)
print(response.json())
```

The response might be:

```
{
    "sentiment": "Positive"
}
```

Key Results and Impact

- **Real-Time Sentiment Analysis**: The system allowed the company to analyze customer reviews instantly as they were posted. This helped the company better understand customer feedback and act on it immediately.
- **Compact and Efficient**: The **DistilBERT** model was

compact, meaning it could be deployed on a cloud platform without the heavy computational requirements of larger models like BERT. This ensured a fast, low-latency experience for real-time applications.

- **Scalability**: As the company grew, the solution could scale to analyze thousands of reviews per day without significant changes to the infrastructure.
- **Improved Customer Experience**: By identifying negative sentiments early, the company could prioritize customer service responses, address issues more effectively, and maintain a positive reputation.
- **Cost-Effective**: The use of a smaller model reduced cloud infrastructure costs compared to deploying larger models. The model's efficiency allowed for real-time sentiment analysis at a lower cost.

Conclusion

This case study highlights how **compact AI models** like **DistilBERT** can be effectively used for real-time applications such as **sentiment analysis** in the e-commerce sector. By deploying a small but powerful model, the company was able to efficiently analyze customer reviews, gain insights into customer satisfaction, and provide timely responses to customer concerns. The approach demonstrated that smaller models could deliver significant value by balancing performance, scalability, and cost-effectiveness.

Case Study: Compact AI for Real-Time Fraud Detection in Financial Transactions

Background:

A global financial services company wanted to implement a **real-time fraud detection system** to monitor and flag suspicious transactions. The goal was to create a system that could quickly analyze financial transaction data, identify potential fraud, and trigger alerts for further investigation—all without the latency and resource consumption typically associated with large machine learning models.

Due to resource constraints, the company required a solution based on **small language models** that could run efficiently on their existing cloud infrastructure. The company selected a **small transformer model** (DistilBERT) for this purpose. DistilBERT is lightweight, fast, and retains a significant portion of the performance of the larger BERT model, making it an ideal candidate for real-time fraud detection.

Solution Approach:

1. **Data Collection**: The financial transactions were gathered, including labels indicating whether a transaction was fraudulent or not.
2. **Model Selection**: A pre-trained **DistilBERT** model was selected and fine-tuned on the fraud detection dataset.
3. **Model Training and Evaluation**: The model was fine-tuned using transaction descriptions and metadata (e.g., amount, location, merchant, etc.).
4. **Deployment**: The model was deployed on the company's cloud infrastructure to analyze new transactions in real time and flag potentially fraudulent ones.

Implementation Details

1. Install Required Libraries

pip install transformers torch scikit-learn Flask pandas

2. Data Preparation

The dataset contains transaction descriptions, metadata (like amount, merchant, etc.), and a fraud label (fraudulent or not).

import pandas as pd

```
# Sample transaction data
data = {
    'transaction_description': [
        'Purchase at electronics store',
        'Payment for groceries',
        'Transfer from bank account',
        'Purchase at online marketplace',
        'Payment for service fee'
    ],
    'transaction_amount': [500, 25, 3000, 150, 200],
    'label': [1, 0, 1, 0, 0]  # 1=fraudulent, 0=non-fraudulent
}

df = pd.DataFrame(data)
```

3. Tokenization and Model Preparation

We tokenize the transaction descriptions and prepare the model for training.

```
from transformers import DistilBertTokenizer

# Load DistilBERT tokenizer
tokenizer = DistilBertTokenizer.from_pretrained('distilbert-base-uncased')

# Tokenize transaction descriptions
inputs = tokenizer(df['transaction_description'].tolist(), padding=True, truncation=True, return_tensors='pt')
labels = torch.tensor(df['label'].tolist())
```

4. Model Setup and Fine-Tuning

We fine-tune the **DistilBERT** model for binary classification (fraudulent or non-fraudulent).

```
from transformers import DistilBertForSequenceClassification, Trainer, TrainingArguments
import torch

# Load DistilBERT for binary classification
model = DistilBertForSequenceClassification.from_pretrained('distilbert-base-uncased', num_labels=2)

# Set up the training arguments
training_args = TrainingArguments(
    output_dir='./results',       # output directory
    num_train_epochs=3,           # number of training epochs
    per_device_train_batch_size=8,  # batch size for training
    logging_dir='./logs',         # directory for storing logs
)

# Initialize Trainer
trainer = Trainer(
    model=model,
    args=training_args,
    train_dataset=torch.utils.data.TensorDataset(inputs['input_ids'], labels),
)

# Fine-tune the model
```

trainer.train()

5. Deploy the Fraud Detection API Using Flask

We create a simple Flask app to serve the model and classify incoming transactions as fraudulent or not.

```
from flask import Flask, request, jsonify

# Initialize Flask app
app = Flask(__name__)

# Load the fine-tuned model
model.eval()

@app.route('/fraud-detection', methods=['POST'])
def fraud_detection():
    # Get the transaction description from the POST request
    transaction_data = request.json
    transaction_description = transaction_data['transaction_description']

    # Tokenize the transaction description
    inputs = tokenizer(transaction_description, return_tensors='pt', padding=True, truncation=True)

    # Get the model's prediction
    with torch.no_grad():
        outputs = model(inputs)
        predicted_class = torch.argmax(outputs.logits, dim=1).item()

    # Map the predicted class to the corresponding label
```

```
    result = 'Fraudulent' if predicted_class == 1 else 'Non-Fraudulent'

    return jsonify({"fraud_status": result})

if __name__ == "__main__":
    app.run(debug=True)
```

6. Testing the Fraud Detection API

You can test the fraud detection API by sending a POST request with a transaction description.

```
import requests

# Send a transaction description to the fraud detection API
url = "http://127.0.0.1:5000/fraud-detection"
transaction = {"transaction_description": "Unusual transfer to foreign account"}

response = requests.post(url, json=transaction)
print(response.json())
```

The response might be:

```
{
    "fraud_status": "Fraudulent"
}
```

Key Results and Impact

- **Real-Time Fraud Detection**: The solution enabled the financial services company to monitor transactions in real time and immediately flag suspicious activities.
- **Compact and Efficient**: Using the **DistilBERT** model allowed the company to deploy a compact yet

effective solution that could analyze transactions quickly without significant computational overhead.

- **Scalability**: The model was able to scale across millions of transactions, enabling the company to process a large number of transactions in real time.
- **Cost-Effective**: By using a smaller model, the company was able to reduce infrastructure costs compared to using larger, more resource-intensive models.
- **Improved Security**: The ability to detect fraudulent transactions in real time helped the company protect its clients and reduce financial losses due to fraud.

Conclusion

This case study demonstrates how **compact AI models**, such as **DistilBERT**, can be effectively used for high-stakes applications like **real-time fraud detection**. The use of small language models provided significant advantages in terms of efficiency, scalability, and cost-effectiveness while maintaining high accuracy. The solution enabled the financial services company to monitor transactions in real time, flagging potentially fraudulent activities and ensuring the security of their clients' financial operations.

Case Study: Compact AI for Real-Time Sentiment Analysis in Social Media Monitoring

Background:

A global marketing firm specializing in social media analytics wanted to implement a **real-time sentiment analysis system** to track public opinion about their clients' brands and products. They needed a solution that could handle a vast amount of social media posts, comments, and reviews quickly, but at the same time, the model should be lightweight and cost-efficient due to resource constraints.

To meet these needs, the firm decided to utilize **small language models** that could run on their cloud infrastructure, providing the needed sentiment analysis capabilities without the overhead of large models. They chose **DistilBERT**, a smaller, faster, and more efficient version of BERT, as it can still capture context and meaning in text while being much more lightweight than its larger counterparts.

Solution Approach:

1. **Data Collection**: The team gathered a dataset of social media posts, comments, and reviews related to various brands and products, including their sentiment labels (positive, negative, neutral).
2. **Model Selection**: **DistilBERT** was selected for its ability to perform well in text classification tasks, including sentiment analysis, while being computationally efficient.
3. **Training and Fine-Tuning**: The team fine-tuned the pre-trained DistilBERT model on their social media dataset.
4. **Deployment**: The trained model was deployed to monitor live social media feeds and classify the sentiment of incoming posts in real-time.

Implementation Details

1. Install Required Libraries

pip install transformers torch Flask pandas

2. Data Preparation

The dataset consists of social media posts, labeled with sentiment (positive, negative, neutral).

import pandas as pd

```
# Sample dataset (for simplicity, we are using a small dataset)
data = {
    'text': [
        'I love this product, it works great!',
        'This is the worst purchase I have ever made.',
        'The product is okay, not bad but not great.',
        'Absolutely fantastic service and delivery.',
        'Totally disappointed with the quality of the product.'
    ],
    'label': [1, 0, 2, 1, 0] # 1=positive, 0=negative, 2=neutral
}

df = pd.DataFrame(data)
```

3. Tokenization and Model Preparation

We will use **DistilBERT** for the sentiment classification task. First, we will tokenize the text data.

```
from transformers import DistilBertTokenizer

# Load DistilBERT tokenizer
tokenizer = DistilBertTokenizer.from_pretrained('distilbert-base-uncased')

# Tokenize the text data
inputs = tokenizer(df['text'].tolist(), padding=True, truncation=True, return_tensors='pt')
labels = torch.tensor(df['label'].tolist())
```

4. Model Setup and Fine-Tuning

Here, we fine-tune a pre-trained DistilBERT model for

sentiment classification.

```
from transformers import
DistilBertForSequenceClassification, Trainer,
TrainingArguments
import torch

# Load DistilBERT for sequence classification
model =
DistilBertForSequenceClassification.from_pretrained('distilbe
rt-base-uncased', num_labels=3)

# Set up the training arguments
training_args = TrainingArguments(
    output_dir='./results',        # output directory
    num_train_epochs=3,            # number of training epochs
    per_device_train_batch_size=8, # batch size for training
    logging_dir='./logs',          # directory for storing logs
)

# Initialize Trainer
trainer = Trainer(
    model=model,
    args=training_args,
    train_dataset=torch.utils.data.TensorDataset(inputs['input
_ids'], labels),
)

# Fine-tune the model
trainer.train()
```

5. Deploy the Sentiment Analysis API Using Flask

We now deploy the sentiment analysis model as a web service using **Flask**, which takes social media posts as input and returns the sentiment classification.

```
from flask import Flask, request, jsonify

# Initialize Flask app
app = Flask(__name__)

# Load the fine-tuned model
model.eval()

@app.route('/sentiment', methods=['POST'])
def sentiment_analysis():
    # Get the user input from the POST request
    user_input = request.json['text']

    # Tokenize the input text
    inputs = tokenizer(user_input, return_tensors='pt',
padding=True, truncation=True)

    # Get the model's prediction
    with torch.no_grad():
        outputs = model(inputs)
        predicted_class = torch.argmax(outputs.logits,
dim=1).item()

    # Map the predicted class to the corresponding sentiment
    sentiment_map = {0: 'Negative', 1: 'Positive', 2: 'Neutral'}
    sentiment = sentiment_map[predicted_class]
```

```
    return jsonify({"sentiment": sentiment})

if __name__ == "__main__":
    app.run(debug=True)
```

6. Testing the Sentiment Analysis API

You can test the sentiment analysis API by sending a POST request with a social media post.

```
import requests

# Send a social media post to the sentiment analysis API
url = "http://127.0.0.1:5000/sentiment"
social_media_post = {"text": "I absolutely love this new gadget!"}

response = requests.post(url, json=social_media_post)
print(response.json())
```

The response might be:

```
{
    "sentiment": "Positive"
}
```

Key Results and Impact

- **Real-Time Sentiment Analysis**: The solution enabled the marketing firm to analyze social media posts in real time, tracking public sentiment about brands and products as they emerge.
- **Compact and Efficient**: By using **DistilBERT**, the firm deployed a lightweight and efficient model, which provided quick sentiment analysis without the need for large computational resources.

- **Scalability**: The system could scale to process millions of social media posts per day, with minimal latency.
- **Cost-Effective**: Using a compact AI model allowed the firm to significantly reduce infrastructure costs compared to using larger models, while still achieving high accuracy and performance.
- **Improved Brand Monitoring**: With real-time sentiment analysis, the firm was able to quickly identify customer pain points, gauge public opinion, and respond to social media crises swiftly.

Conclusion

This case study demonstrates how **compact AI models** like **DistilBERT** can be effectively deployed for real-time applications, such as sentiment analysis for social media monitoring. The solution was not only efficient and cost-effective but also scalable, making it an ideal choice for the marketing firm to enhance its social media analytics capabilities. By utilizing small models, they were able to process vast amounts of social media data with minimal computational resources, while still achieving high-quality insights.

Case Study: Compact AI for Customer Support Chatbot in E-Commerce

Background:

An e-commerce platform that specializes in consumer electronics wanted to enhance its customer service experience by integrating an AI-powered chatbot capable of answering common customer queries. The challenge was to implement a **small AI model** that could handle high volumes of inquiries, including product information, order status, and general support questions, while being lightweight enough to run on the cloud with limited resources.

After evaluating several AI models, the team decided to use **DistilBERT**, a smaller and more efficient version of BERT, for this task. The chatbot had to be fast and accurate in understanding natural language, while providing responses to frequently asked questions (FAQs) and resolving basic customer issues.

Solution Approach:

1. **Data Collection**: The team gathered a dataset of frequently asked questions (FAQs) and customer support transcripts related to product inquiries, order issues, and general customer service requests.
2. **Model Selection**: **DistilBERT** was chosen due to its efficiency, smaller size, and ability to perform well on NLP tasks such as question answering.
3. **Data Preprocessing**: The dataset was cleaned and preprocessed for training, including tokenization and encoding of customer queries and responses.
4. **Real-Time Deployment**: The solution was deployed to run on the platform's backend, enabling real-time interactions with customers via a chatbot interface.
5. **Optimization**: The model was fine-tuned on the FAQ dataset to improve accuracy and response time.

Implementation Details

1. Install Required Libraries

pip install transformers torch Flask

2. Data Collection: Prepare FAQ Dataset

For simplicity, we assume a small dataset of FAQs with corresponding responses.

faq_data = {

```
"What are the store hours?": "Our store is open from 9 AM to 9 PM every day.",
"How can I track my order?": "You can track your order status by logging into your account and going to the 'Orders' section.",
"Do you offer international shipping?": "Yes, we ship internationally. Please check our shipping policies for more details.",
"How can I return a product?": "You can return a product within 30 days of purchase. Please visit our returns page for instructions.",
}
```

3. Data Preprocessing: Tokenizing the FAQ Dataset

We will tokenize the questions and their corresponding answers.

```
from transformers import DistilBertTokenizer

# Load the pre-trained DistilBERT tokenizer
tokenizer = DistilBertTokenizer.from_pretrained('distilbert-base-uncased')

# Tokenize questions from the FAQ dataset
questions = list(faq_data.keys())
answers = list(faq_data.values())

encoded_questions = tokenizer(questions, padding=True, truncation=True, return_tensors="pt")
```

4. Model Setup and Fine-Tuning

We use a **DistilBERT model** pre-trained for sequence classification or question answering and fine-tune it on our FAQ dataset. In this case, we'll use a simple **text classification**

model.

```
from transformers import
DistilBertForSequenceClassification, Trainer,
TrainingArguments
import torch

# Define the model
model =
DistilBertForSequenceClassification.from_pretrained('distilbe
rt-base-uncased', num_labels=len(faq_data))

# Prepare inputs and labels for training
inputs = tokenizer(questions, padding=True,
truncation=True, return_tensors="pt")
labels = torch.tensor([i for i in range(len(faq_data))])

# Set up the training arguments
training_args = TrainingArguments(
    output_dir='./results',        # output directory
    num_train_epochs=3,            # number of training epochs
    per_device_train_batch_size=8,  # batch size for training
    logging_dir='./logs',          # directory for storing logs
)

# Initialize Trainer
trainer = Trainer(
    model=model,
    args=training_args,
    train_dataset=torch.utils.data.TensorDataset(inputs['input
```

```
_ids'], labels),
)

# Fine-tune the model
trainer.train()
```

5. Deploy the Chatbot Using Flask

Once the model is trained, we deploy it as a simple chatbot using **Flask** to provide an interface for customer inquiries.

```
from flask import Flask, request, jsonify

# Initialize Flask app
app = Flask(__name__)

# Load the fine-tuned model for inference
model.eval()

@app.route('/chatbot', methods=['POST'])
def chatbot_response():
    # Get user query from POST request
    user_query = request.json['query']

    # Tokenize the user's query
    inputs = tokenizer(user_query, padding=True,
truncation=True, return_tensors="pt")

    # Get the model's prediction
    with torch.no_grad():
        outputs = model(inputs)
        predicted_class = torch.argmax(outputs.logits,
```

```
dim=1).item()

    # Get the corresponding answer from the FAQ dataset
    response = faq_data[questions[predicted_class]]

    # Return the response as JSON
    return jsonify({"response": response})

if __name__ == "__main__":
    app.run(debug=True)
```

6. Testing the Chatbot

You can now test the chatbot by sending a POST request to the Flask server with a user query. For example, you could use **Postman** or Python's requests library.

```
import requests

# Send a query to the chatbot
url = "http://127.0.0.1:5000/chatbot"
query = {"query": "How can I track my order?"}

response = requests.post(url, json=query)
print(response.json())
```

The output might be:

```
{
    "response": "You can track your order status by logging into your account and going to the 'Orders' section."
}
```

Key Results and Impact

- **Real-Time Customer Support**: The chatbot now

provides instant, automated responses to customers' frequently asked questions, reducing the workload on customer service agents.

- **Compact and Efficient**: The model, **DistilBERT**, provided a lightweight solution that could be easily deployed on the backend with limited computational resources.
- **Scalability**: The solution could be scaled to handle various other customer queries, as new FAQs could be added without retraining the entire model.
- **Cost-Efficiency**: By leveraging a smaller model, the company reduced infrastructure costs compared to using larger models while still maintaining a high level of accuracy and response speed.
- **Improved Customer Experience**: The solution enabled the company to provide 24/7 support, enhancing customer satisfaction and enabling customers to get quick answers to their questions.

Conclusion

This case study demonstrates how **compact AI models** like **DistilBERT** can be deployed in practical applications such as e-commerce customer support. The solution was efficient, scalable, and cost-effective, while still providing high-quality responses. By using a small model, the company was able to create a real-time, AI-powered chatbot that significantly enhanced its customer service operations.

Case Study: Compact AI for Real-Time Sentiment Analysis in Social Media Monitoring

Background:

A social media analytics company wanted to build a real-time sentiment analysis tool to monitor brand mentions, customer feedback, and public opinions across platforms like Twitter, Instagram, and Facebook. The challenge was to deploy a **compact AI model** that could handle large volumes of text data and deliver sentiment analysis results in real time with minimal computational overhead.

The company chose to implement a **small transformer model** like **DistilBERT** due to its small size and ability to perform well on NLP tasks such as sentiment analysis.

Solution Approach:

1. **Data Collection**: The company collected social media posts, tweets, and user comments related to various brands.
2. **Model Selection**: **DistilBERT**, a compact version of BERT, was selected for its ability to efficiently handle sentiment analysis while maintaining high accuracy.
3. **Data Preprocessing**: The posts and tweets were preprocessed, cleaned, and tokenized for analysis.
4. **Real-Time Deployment**: The solution was deployed to run continuously on the cloud, monitoring social media streams and providing instant sentiment scores.
5. **Optimization**: The model was fine-tuned on a sentiment-labeled dataset for better accuracy in the context of social media language.

Implementation Details

1. Install Required Libraries

pip install transformers torch tweepy scikit-learn

2. Data Collection: Pull Tweets Using Tweepy

To simulate a real-time application, the company used **Tweepy** to pull tweets from Twitter using keywords related to brand names.

```
import tweepy

# Set up Tweepy credentials (you must use your own keys here)
consumer_key = 'YOUR_CONSUMER_KEY'
consumer_secret = 'YOUR_CONSUMER_SECRET'
access_token = 'YOUR_ACCESS_TOKEN'
access_token_secret = 'YOUR_ACCESS_TOKEN_SECRET'

# Set up API connection
auth = tweepy.OAuthHandler(consumer_key, consumer_secret)
auth.set_access_token(access_token, access_token_secret)
api = tweepy.API(auth)

# Fetch tweets mentioning a brand
tweets = api.search_tweets(q="BrandName", lang="en", count=100)

# Extract tweet texts
tweet_texts = [tweet.text for tweet in tweets]
```

3. Preprocess the Data for Sentiment Analysis

We use the **DistilBERT tokenizer** to tokenize the tweets and prepare them for sentiment analysis.

```
from transformers import DistilBertTokenizer

# Load the pre-trained DistilBERT tokenizer
tokenizer = DistilBertTokenizer.from_pretrained('distilbert-base-uncased')

# Tokenize the tweets
```

```
def preprocess_tweet(tweets, tokenizer, max_length=128):
    return tokenizer(tweets, padding=True, truncation=True, max_length=max_length)

encoded_tweets = preprocess_tweet(tweet_texts, tokenizer)
```

4. Sentiment Analysis with DistilBERT

We now load the pre-trained **DistilBERT model** and fine-tune it on a sentiment analysis dataset (if necessary). In this case, we will use the pipeline API from Hugging Face to make sentiment predictions.

```
from transformers import DistilBertForSequenceClassification, pipeline
import torch

# Load the pre-trained DistilBERT model for sentiment analysis
model = DistilBertForSequenceClassification.from_pretrained('distilbert-base-uncased', num_labels=2)

# Load the sentiment analysis pipeline
sentiment_analysis = pipeline('sentiment-analysis', model=model, tokenizer=tokenizer)

# Run sentiment analysis on the tokenized tweets
sentiment_results = sentiment_analysis(tweet_texts)

# Display the results
for i, result in enumerate(sentiment_results):
    print(f"Tweet {i+1}: {tweet_texts[i]}")
    print(f"Sentiment: {result['label']}, Confidence:
```

```
{result['score']}\n")
```

5. Real-Time Sentiment Analysis on New Tweets

To simulate real-time sentiment analysis, we continuously monitor Twitter for new tweets and apply sentiment analysis to each tweet in real time.

```
import time

# Function to fetch and analyze new tweets
def real_time_sentiment_analysis(api, sentiment_pipeline, query="BrandName", count=100):
    # Fetch new tweets
    tweets = api.search_tweets(q=query, lang="en", count=count)
    tweet_texts = [tweet.text for tweet in tweets]

    # Perform sentiment analysis on new tweets
    sentiment_results = sentiment_pipeline(tweet_texts)

    # Display results
    for i, result in enumerate(sentiment_results):
        print(f"Tweet {i+1}: {tweet_texts[i]}")
        print(f"Sentiment: {result['label']}, Confidence: {result['score']}\n")

# Simulate real-time processing by running every 10 seconds
while True:
    real_time_sentiment_analysis(api, sentiment_analysis)
    time.sleep(10) # Adjust frequency of updates
```

Key Results and Impact

- **Real-Time Monitoring**: The system enabled real-time sentiment analysis of social media posts and tweets, providing immediate insights into customer opinions and brand perceptions.
- **Compact and Efficient**: Using **DistilBERT**, the model was able to process a large volume of tweets with minimal latency, making it suitable for real-time deployment.
- **Scalable**: The solution could easily scale to monitor multiple brands simultaneously by modifying the search keywords and using cloud resources.
- **Actionable Insights**: The sentiment analysis allowed the company to quickly identify positive and negative sentiments, enabling brands to respond proactively to customer feedback.
- **Cost-Effective**: By using a compact model, the company reduced infrastructure costs compared to using larger models, making the system more cost-efficient while still delivering accurate results.

Conclusion

This case study highlights how **compact AI models** like **DistilBERT** can be effectively used for real-time sentiment analysis in social media monitoring. The solution was lightweight, scalable, and efficient, allowing the company to gain actionable insights from social media platforms without heavy computational resources. By leveraging small models, the company was able to enhance its brand monitoring system and improve its ability to respond to customer feedback in real time.

Case Study: Compact AI for Real-Time Product Recommendations

Background:

A leading e-commerce platform wanted to improve its product recommendation system. The goal was to provide personalized recommendations to customers based on their browsing history, previous purchases, and preferences. The challenge was to implement a solution using **small language models** that would allow real-time, personalized recommendations with minimal computational resources.

The company chose to use a **small transformer-based model** like **DistilBERT** for its efficiency and ability to handle complex text data such as product descriptions, reviews, and user queries.

Solution Approach:

1. **Data Collection**: The company collected data from customer browsing history, product descriptions, and user reviews.
2. **Model Selection**: A **DistilBERT** model was chosen for its lightweight architecture, making it suitable for real-time inference.
3. **Feature Extraction**: Product descriptions and customer preferences were encoded into embeddings using the model.
4. **Recommendation Engine**: The embeddings were used to match products with user profiles, generating personalized product recommendations.
5. **Real-Time Deployment**: The solution was deployed in the cloud for scalable real-time recommendations.

Implementation Details

1. Install Required Libraries

pip install transformers torch scikit-learn

2. Data Preprocessing

Assuming we have a dataset with customer browsing history and product details, we need to preprocess the data for the recommendation engine.

```
import pandas as pd
from transformers import DistilBertTokenizer

# Sample customer browsing data and product descriptions
data = {
    'customer_id': [1, 2, 3, 4],
    'browsing_history': [
        'laptop gaming', 'smartphone', 'headphones wireless',
'gaming chair'
    ],
    'product_id': [101, 102, 103, 104],
    'product_description': [
        'High performance gaming laptop with latest specs.',
        'Latest smartphone with advanced features.',
        'Noise cancelling wireless headphones.',
        'Comfortable and ergonomic gaming chair.'
    ]
}

df = pd.DataFrame(data)

# Tokenizer initialization
tokenizer = DistilBertTokenizer.from_pretrained('distilbert-
base-uncased')

# Preprocess product descriptions and browsing history
```

```
def preprocess_data(texts, tokenizer, max_length=128):
    return tokenizer(texts, padding=True, truncation=True, max_length=max_length)

# Tokenize the product descriptions and browsing history
product_encodings = preprocess_data(df['product_description'].tolist(), tokenizer)
history_encodings = preprocess_data(df['browsing_history'].tolist(), tokenizer)
```

3. Product and User Embedding Extraction

We will extract embeddings for both product descriptions and customer browsing history using the **DistilBERT** model.

```
import torch
from transformers import DistilBertModel

# Load the pre-trained DistilBERT model for embeddings
model = DistilBertModel.from_pretrained('distilbert-base-uncased')

# Function to get embeddings from DistilBERT
def get_embeddings(encodings, model):
    with torch.no_grad():
        outputs = model(encodings)
    return outputs.last_hidden_state.mean(dim=1)  # Average pool the token embeddings

# Get product embeddings
product_embeddings = get_embeddings(product_encodings, model)
```

```
# Get browsing history embeddings for customers
history_embeddings = get_embeddings(history_encodings, model)
```

4. Calculating Similarity and Generating Recommendations

To generate recommendations, we calculate the **cosine similarity** between customer browsing history embeddings and product description embeddings. The products with the highest similarity scores are recommended.

```
from sklearn.metrics.pairwise import cosine_similarity

# Calculate cosine similarity between product embeddings and customer browsing history embeddings
similarities = cosine_similarity(history_embeddings, product_embeddings)

# Generate recommendations for each customer
def generate_recommendations(similarities, num_recommendations=3):
    recommendations = {}
    for i, similarity in enumerate(similarities):
        recommended_product_indices = similarity.argsort()[-num_recommendations:][::-1]
        recommendations[i] = recommended_product_indices.tolist()
    return recommendations

# Generate top 3 recommendations for each customer
recommendations = generate_recommendations(similarities)
```

5. Display Recommendations

Finally, we display the top 3 recommended products for each customer.

```
# Display recommendations
for customer_id, recommended_product_indices in recommendations.items():
    print(f"Recommendations for Customer {df['customer_id'][customer_id]}:")
    for product_index in recommended_product_indices:
        print(f"- Product ID: {df['product_id'][product_index]}, Description: {df['product_description'][product_index]}")
    print("\n")
```

Key Results and Impact

- **Real-Time Recommendations**: The compact model enabled the company to generate personalized product recommendations in real-time, providing a better shopping experience for customers.
- **Scalability**: Using **DistilBERT**, the company was able to handle large amounts of product data and customer interactions without overwhelming computational resources.
- **Improved Customer Engagement**: Personalized recommendations led to an increase in customer engagement, as users were more likely to purchase products that matched their interests.
- **Enhanced Product Discovery**: Customers were introduced to new products that they might not have discovered on their own, boosting sales.

Conclusion

This case study demonstrates how **compact AI models**, such as **DistilBERT**, can be effectively applied in e-commerce platforms for real-time product recommendation systems. The solution was able to deliver personalized recommendations at scale while minimizing computational costs. By utilizing small language models, the company was able to provide a richer and more personalized customer experience, improving customer satisfaction and driving higher conversion rates.

Case Study: Compact AI for Sentiment Analysis in Customer Feedback

Background:

A global retail company wanted to improve its customer satisfaction by analyzing customer feedback from various sources, such as product reviews, customer surveys, and social media comments. The company needed a solution to automatically assess the sentiment of feedback, categorize it (positive, neutral, or negative), and identify key areas for improvement.

The challenge was to implement this solution using a **small language model** that could run efficiently on edge devices and handle a large volume of customer feedback data in real-time.

The company opted for a **small transformer-based model** like **DistilBERT**, which is known for its performance efficiency while maintaining high accuracy in tasks like sentiment analysis.

Solution Approach:

1. **Data Collection**: The company gathered data from multiple sources, including customer reviews, survey responses, and social media.
2. **Model Selection**: A **DistilBERT** model was selected, which was fine-tuned on sentiment-labeled data.
3. **Fine-Tuning**: The model was fine-tuned using labeled customer feedback data for sentiment

classification.

4. **Real-Time Sentiment Classification**: The trained model was deployed to classify incoming feedback into positive, neutral, or negative categories in real-time.
5. **Deployment**: The solution was deployed to the cloud to handle millions of feedback data points, ensuring it could scale with increasing customer feedback.

Implementation Details

1. Install Required Libraries

```
pip install transformers torch scikit-learn
```

2. Data Preprocessing

Assuming we have a dataset consisting of customer feedback and sentiment labels (positive, negative, or neutral), the next step is to preprocess the data.

```
import pandas as pd
from sklearn.model_selection import train_test_split
from transformers import DistilBertTokenizer

# Sample customer feedback dataset
data = {
    'feedback': [
        'I love the new product! It works perfectly.',
        'The delivery was delayed, and the product was damaged.',
        'Great experience overall, but the customer service could be improved.',
        'The product did not meet my expectations.',
        'Absolutely fantastic! I will recommend it to my friends.'
```

```
],
'sentiment': ['positive', 'negative', 'neutral', 'negative', 'positive']
}

df = pd.DataFrame(data)

# Tokenizer initialization
tokenizer = DistilBertTokenizer.from_pretrained('distilbert-base-uncased')

# Preprocess the feedback text
def preprocess_data(texts, tokenizer, max_length=128):
    return tokenizer(texts, padding=True, truncation=True, max_length=max_length)

# Tokenize the feedback data
feedback_encodings = preprocess_data(df['feedback'].tolist(), tokenizer)

# Convert sentiment labels to numerical values
sentiment_map = {'positive': 0, 'neutral': 1, 'negative': 2}
df['sentiment_label'] = df['sentiment'].map(sentiment_map)

# Split dataset into training and testing sets
train_data, test_data = train_test_split(df, test_size=0.2)
```

3. Model Fine-Tuning

We'll use **DistilBERT** for sequence classification (sentiment analysis). Fine-tuning the model involves training it with the feedback dataset.

```
from transformers import DistilBertForSequenceClassification, Trainer, TrainingArguments
import torch

# Define the custom dataset class for sentiment classification
class FeedbackSentimentDataset(torch.utils.data.Dataset):
    def __init__(self, feedback, labels, encodings):
        self.feedback = feedback
        self.labels = labels
        self.encodings = encodings

    def __getitem__(self, idx):
        item = {key: torch.tensor(val[idx]) for key, val in self.encodings.items()}
        item['labels'] = torch.tensor(self.labels[idx])
        return item

    def __len__(self):
        return len(self.labels)

# Prepare the datasets for training and evaluation
train_dataset = FeedbackSentimentDataset(train_data['feedback'], train_data['sentiment_label'], feedback_encodings)
test_dataset = FeedbackSentimentDataset(test_data['feedback'], test_data['sentiment_label'], feedback_encodings)

# Initialize the model for sentiment classification
```

```
model =
DistilBertForSequenceClassification.from_pretrained('distilbe
rt-base-uncased', num_labels=len(sentiment_map))

# Set training arguments
training_args = TrainingArguments(
    output_dir='./results',
    num_train_epochs=3,
    per_device_train_batch_size=8,
    per_device_eval_batch_size=16,
    warmup_steps=500,
    weight_decay=0.01,
    logging_dir='./logs',
)

# Initialize Trainer
trainer = Trainer(
    model=model,
    args=training_args,
    train_dataset=train_dataset,
    eval_dataset=test_dataset,
)

# Fine-tune the model
trainer.train()
```

4. Model Evaluation

After training, evaluate the model's performance on the test data.

```
# Evaluate the fine-tuned model
trainer.evaluate()
```

5. Real-Time Sentiment Analysis

Once the model is trained, it can be used to classify new customer feedback in real-time.

```
# Function to predict sentiment from customer feedback
def predict_sentiment(feedback, model, tokenizer):
    # Preprocess the feedback text
    encoded_input = tokenizer(feedback, return_tensors="pt", padding=True, truncation=True, max_length=128)

    # Get the model's prediction (sentiment category)
    with torch.no_grad():
        outputs = model(encoded_input)
        logits = outputs.logits
        predicted_class = torch.argmax(logits, dim=1).item()

    # Retrieve the sentiment label (map the predicted class to sentiment)
    sentiment = list(sentiment_map.keys())[predicted_class]
    return sentiment

# Test with a new piece of feedback
new_feedback = "The service was excellent, but the product quality could be improved."
predicted_sentiment = predict_sentiment(new_feedback, model, tokenizer)
print(f"Predicted Sentiment: {predicted_sentiment}")
```

6. Optimizing for Deployment

For deployment in a cloud environment, the model can be converted to **ONNX** format for faster inference.

```
# Convert the model to ONNX format
onnx_path = 'sentiment_analysis_model.onnx'
dummy_input = torch.ones(1, 128, dtype=torch.long) # 1 example, 128 tokens

# Export the model to ONNX
torch.onnx.export(model, dummy_input, onnx_path, export_params=True, opset_version=12)
```

Key Results and Impact

- **Real-time Sentiment Classification**: The sentiment analysis model allows the company to analyze customer feedback in real-time, improving response time and customer satisfaction.
- **Efficiency and Scalability**: Using the **DistilBERT** model, the company built a lightweight solution capable of processing large volumes of feedback without overwhelming computational resources.
- **Improved Customer Insights**: By categorizing feedback into positive, neutral, and negative sentiments, the company gained better insights into customer preferences, allowing them to respond proactively.
- **Enhanced Customer Experience**: By automating sentiment analysis, the company was able to handle customer feedback faster and with greater accuracy, improving the overall customer experience.

Conclusion

This case study demonstrates how compact AI models like **DistilBERT** can be effectively used for real-time sentiment analysis in customer feedback systems. By leveraging the power of small language models, the retail company was able to build a highly efficient solution that provides valuable insights into customer satisfaction, leading to better decision-making and enhanced customer experience.

Case Study: Compact AI for E-commerce Product Recommendation System

Background:

An e-commerce platform wanted to enhance its product recommendation system to improve customer engagement and sales. The company wanted a system capable of recommending products in real-time based on user preferences, browsing history, and purchase data. The challenge was to build a recommendation system using a **small language model** that could run efficiently on edge devices with limited computational resources, while still providing high-quality and personalized product suggestions.

Given these constraints, the company chose to implement a **small transformer model—DistilBERT**, a lighter version of BERT. This model was selected for its ability to process textual data (like product descriptions, reviews, and search queries) with high accuracy while being computationally efficient.

Solution Approach:

The solution was built by integrating the following components:

1. **Data Collection**: The platform collected data from customer searches, product views, and previous purchases to train the recommendation model.
2. **Model Selection**: **DistilBERT** was chosen as the base model, which was fine-tuned for generating product recommendations.
3. **Fine-Tuning**: The DistilBERT model was fine-tuned

with the product dataset, including features like product names, descriptions, and customer reviews.

4. **Recommendation Generation**: The fine-tuned model generated product recommendations based on the customer's behavior.
5. **Deployment**: The model was deployed in an online environment with a cloud back-end, capable of real-time recommendation for thousands of customers.

Implementation Details

1. Install Required Libraries

First, ensure the necessary Python libraries are installed.

```
pip install transformers torch scikit-learn
```

2. Data Preprocessing

For simplicity, assume the dataset consists of product descriptions, customer reviews, and past purchase data. We will use the **DistilBERT tokenizer** to preprocess text data.

```
import pandas as pd

from sklearn.model_selection import train_test_split

from transformers import DistilBertTokenizer


# Sample dataset (Product Name, Description, Customer Review, Target Product Category)

data = {

    'product_name': ['Wireless Mouse', 'Gaming Laptop', 'Smartphone', 'Bluetooth Headphones', 'Smartwatch'],

    'product_description': [

        'A wireless mouse with ergonomic design and long battery life.',

        'High performance gaming laptop with RTX 3080 GPU and 16GB RAM.',
```

```
        'Latest smartphone with a 108MP camera and 5G connectivity.',
        'Over-ear Bluetooth headphones with noise cancellation.',
        'Smartwatch with heart rate monitor and fitness tracking.'
    ],
    'customer_review': [
        'Very comfortable and precise mouse, great for long hours of work.',
        'Perfect for gaming, runs all modern games smoothly.',
        'Excellent phone with amazing camera quality, highly recommend.',
        'Great sound quality and comfort for long listening sessions.',
        'Works great for fitness tracking, but the screen is small.'
    ],
    'target_category': ['Electronics', 'Computers', 'Mobile', 'Audio', 'Wearables']
}

df = pd.DataFrame(data)

# Tokenizer initialization
tokenizer = DistilBertTokenizer.from_pretrained('distilbert-base-uncased')

# Preprocess the product descriptions and customer reviews
def preprocess_data(texts, tokenizer, max_length=128):
    return tokenizer(texts, padding=True, truncation=True,
```

```
max_length=max_length)

# Tokenize the data
product_desc_encodings = preprocess_data(df['product_description'].tolist(), tokenizer)
customer_review_encodings = preprocess_data(df['customer_review'].tolist(), tokenizer)

# Convert categories to labels
category_map = {category: idx for idx, category in enumerate(df['target_category'].unique())}
df['category_label'] = df['target_category'].map(category_map)

# Split dataset into training and testing sets
train_data, test_data = train_test_split(df, test_size=0.2)
```

3. Model Fine-Tuning

Now, we'll fine-tune **DistilBERT** to predict the most relevant product category for each review or description. This is a simplified approach to a recommendation system, where we treat it as a classification problem based on product descriptions and reviews.

```
from transformers import DistilBertForSequenceClassification, Trainer, TrainingArguments
import torch

# Define custom dataset class
class ProductRecommendationDataset(torch.utils.data.Dataset):
    def __init__(self, descriptions, reviews, labels, desc_encodings, review_encodings):
```

```
        self.descriptions = descriptions
        self.reviews = reviews
        self.labels = labels
        self.desc_encodings = desc_encodings
        self.review_encodings = review_encodings

    def __getitem__(self, idx):
        desc_item = {key: torch.tensor(val[idx]) for key, val in
self.desc_encodings.items()}
        review_item = {key: torch.tensor(val[idx]) for key, val in
self.review_encodings.items()}

        # Concatenate description and review features for the
input to the model
        inputs = {key: torch.cat((desc_item[key],
review_item[key]), dim=-1) for key in desc_item}

        # Labels for classification task
        inputs['labels'] = torch.tensor(self.labels[idx])

        return inputs

    def __len__(self):
        return len(self.labels)

# Prepare the datasets
train_dataset =
ProductRecommendationDataset(train_data['product_descrip
tion'], train_data['customer_review'],
                                    train_data['category_label'],
```

```
product_desc_encodings, customer_review_encodings)
test_dataset                                                  =
ProductRecommendationDataset(test_data['product_descript
ion'], test_data['customer_review'],
                                   test_data['category_label'],
product_desc_encodings, customer_review_encodings)

# Initialize the model for sequence classification
model                                                         =
DistilBertForSequenceClassification.from_pretrained('distilbe
rt-base-uncased', num_labels=len(category_map))

# Set training arguments
training_args = TrainingArguments(
    output_dir='./results',
    num_train_epochs=3,
    per_device_train_batch_size=8,
    per_device_eval_batch_size=16,
    warmup_steps=500,
    weight_decay=0.01,
    logging_dir='./logs',
)

# Initialize Trainer
trainer = Trainer(
    model=model,
    args=training_args,
    train_dataset=train_dataset,
    eval_dataset=test_dataset,
```

```
)

# Fine-tune the model
trainer.train()
```

4. Model Evaluation

Evaluate the fine-tuned model's accuracy on the test dataset.

```
# Evaluate the model
trainer.evaluate()
```

5. Real-Time Recommendation

Once the model is trained, it can be used for real-time product recommendations. Given a customer's review or description, the model will predict the product category, suggesting relevant products.

```
# Function to get product recommendations based on customer review
def recommend_product(review, model, tokenizer):
    # Preprocess the review and description
    encoded_input = tokenizer(review, return_tensors="pt", padding=True, truncation=True, max_length=128)

    # Get the model's prediction (product category)
    with torch.no_grad():
        outputs = model(encoded_input)
        logits = outputs.logits
        predicted_class = torch.argmax(logits, dim=1).item()

    # Retrieve product recommendation (mapping to the category)
    recommended_category = list(category_map.keys())
```

```
[predicted_class]
    return recommended_category

# Test with a new customer review
new_review = "I want a phone that is fast and has a good camera."
recommended_category = recommend_product(new_review, model, tokenizer)
print(f"Recommended Product Category: {recommended_category}")
```

6. Optimizing for Deployment

For real-time prediction, the model can be converted into an optimized format like **ONNX** for faster inference.

```
# Convert the model to ONNX format
onnx_path = 'product_recommendation_model.onnx'
dummy_input = torch.ones(1, 128, dtype=torch.long)  # 1 example, 128 tokens

# Export the model
torch.onnx.export(model, dummy_input, onnx_path, export_params=True, opset_version=12)
```

Key Results and Impact

- **Personalized Recommendations**: The system provides personalized product recommendations based on customer reviews and descriptions, enhancing the shopping experience.
- **Efficiency**: By using **DistilBERT**, the system is computationally efficient, making it suitable for real-time use in a cloud environment with limited resources.

- **Improved Engagement**: Customers received better product suggestions, which improved engagement and increased sales.
- **Scalability**: The system can scale across thousands of customers and products, handling millions of interactions with low latency.

Conclusion

This case study demonstrates how small, compact models like **DistilBERT** can be leveraged in real-world applications like product recommendation systems. By using a lightweight AI model, the e-commerce platform was able to provide personalized recommendations in real time without compromising on efficiency or quality. This shows that small language models can play a crucial role in driving business success, especially in resource-constrained environments.

Case Study: Compact AI for Sentiment Analysis in Social Media Monitoring

Background:

A marketing analytics firm aimed to enhance its brand monitoring platform by integrating sentiment analysis to gauge public sentiment about brands in real-time. The platform needs to monitor vast amounts of social media content, including Twitter posts and Facebook comments, to analyze customer feelings and adjust marketing strategies. However, the client's primary requirement was that the sentiment analysis model be lightweight enough to run efficiently on a cloud platform with limited resources.

Given these constraints, the firm chose a **small language model** approach using **TinyBERT** (a compact version of BERT). This decision was based on the model's ability to perform sentiment analysis tasks while keeping the computational overhead low.

Solution Approach:

The process for building the sentiment analysis system was broken into the following steps:

1. **Data Collection**: The firm collected a large dataset of social media posts labeled with sentiment labels (positive, negative, and neutral).
2. **Model Selection**: **TinyBERT**, a smaller, more efficient version of BERT, was chosen for sentiment analysis.
3. **Fine-Tuning**: TinyBERT was fine-tuned on the sentiment-labeled dataset.
4. **Deployment**: The fine-tuned model was deployed on the cloud to analyze posts in real-time, identifying the overall sentiment towards brands.
5. **Real-Time Prediction**: The system is capable of providing real-time sentiment analysis as new posts are published.

Implementation Details

1. Install Required Libraries

First, we need to install the required Python libraries.

```
pip install transformers torch
```

2. Data Preprocessing

We'll use a small, labeled dataset of social media posts with sentiments to fine-tune the TinyBERT model. Let's assume we have three classes: **positive**, **negative**, and **neutral**.

```
import pandas as pd

from sklearn.model_selection import train_test_split

from transformers import BertTokenizer


# Example dataset with social media posts and their corresponding sentiments
```

```
data = {
    'text': ['I love the new phone!', 'This product is terrible.', 'The customer service is just okay.',
             'Amazing experience with the brand!', 'I'm never buying this again.', 'The product was fine.'],
    'sentiment': ['positive', 'negative', 'neutral', 'positive', 'negative', 'neutral']
}

df = pd.DataFrame(data)

# Split dataset into training and testing sets
train_data, test_data = train_test_split(df, test_size=0.2)

# Initialize the TinyBERT tokenizer
tokenizer = BertTokenizer.from_pretrained('google/tinybert-l12')

# Preprocess the data by tokenizing the texts
def preprocess_data(texts, tokenizer, max_length=64):
    return tokenizer(texts, padding=True, truncation=True, max_length=max_length)

# Tokenize the training and testing data
train_encodings = preprocess_data(train_data['text'].tolist(), tokenizer)
test_encodings = preprocess_data(test_data['text'].tolist(), tokenizer)

# Convert sentiments to integer labels
```

```
sentiment_map = {'positive': 0, 'negative': 1, 'neutral': 2}
train_labels = train_data['sentiment'].map(sentiment_map).tolist()
test_labels = test_data['sentiment'].map(sentiment_map).tolist()
```

3. Model Fine-Tuning

We will fine-tune the **TinyBERT** model on our sentiment dataset.

```
from transformers import BertForSequenceClassification, Trainer, TrainingArguments
import torch

# Define a custom dataset class for PyTorch
class SentimentDataset(torch.utils.data.Dataset):
    def __init__(self, encodings, labels):
        self.encodings = encodings
        self.labels = labels

    def __getitem__(self, idx):
        item = {key: torch.tensor(val[idx]) for key, val in self.encodings.items()}
        item['labels'] = torch.tensor(self.labels[idx])
        return item

    def __len__(self):
        return len(self.labels)

# Create training and testing datasets
train_dataset = SentimentDataset(train_encodings,
```

```
train_labels)
test_dataset = SentimentDataset(test_encodings, test_labels)

# Load TinyBERT for sequence classification
model                                                        =
BertForSequenceClassification.from_pretrained('google/
tinybert-l12', num_labels=len(sentiment_map))

# Set up training arguments
training_args = TrainingArguments(
    output_dir='./results',
    num_train_epochs=3,
    per_device_train_batch_size=16,
    per_device_eval_batch_size=64,
    warmup_steps=500,
    weight_decay=0.01,
    logging_dir='./logs',
    logging_steps=10,
)

# Initialize Trainer
trainer = Trainer(
    model=model,
    args=training_args,
    train_dataset=train_dataset,
    eval_dataset=test_dataset,
)
```

```
# Fine-tune the model
trainer.train()
```

4. Model Evaluation

After training, we evaluate the model's performance on the test dataset.

```
# Evaluate the model on the test dataset
trainer.evaluate()
```

5. Real-Time Sentiment Prediction

Now that the model is fine-tuned, we can use it to predict the sentiment of new social media posts.

```
# Function to predict sentiment of a new social media post
def predict_sentiment(post, model, tokenizer):
    inputs = tokenizer(post, return_tensors="pt", truncation=True, padding=True, max_length=64)
    outputs = model(inputs)
    logits = outputs.logits
    predicted_label = torch.argmax(logits, dim=1).item()
    return list(sentiment_map.keys())[predicted_label]

# Test with a new social media post
new_post = "I love this new phone! It's amazing."
predicted_sentiment = predict_sentiment(new_post, model, tokenizer)
print(f"Predicted Sentiment: {predicted_sentiment}")
```

6. Optimizing for Deployment

To deploy this model on a cloud platform or edge device, it can be converted to **ONNX** format for faster inference.

```
import torch.onnx
```

```
# Convert the model to ONNX format
onnx_path = 'sentiment_analysis_model.onnx'
dummy_input = torch.ones(1, 64, dtype=torch.long)  # 1 example, 64 tokens

# Export the model to ONNX
torch.onnx.export(model, dummy_input, onnx_path, export_params=True, opset_version=12)
```

Key Results and Impact

- **Real-Time Monitoring**: The sentiment analysis system can now analyze large volumes of social media content in real time. It helps the marketing team to gauge public sentiment instantly.
- **Resource Efficiency**: By using **TinyBERT**, the solution operates efficiently on cloud services with limited resources, making it cost-effective and scalable.
- **Accuracy**: The model accurately predicts sentiment (positive, negative, or neutral) in the context of social media posts, enabling the firm to quickly identify trends and customer reactions.
- **Scalability**: This approach is scalable for monitoring large social media platforms, providing actionable insights across multiple brands simultaneously.

Conclusion

This case study demonstrates how small, efficient models like **TinyBERT** can be applied to real-time tasks such as sentiment analysis on social media. By using compact AI, the company was able to deploy a highly effective, resource-efficient solution for monitoring customer sentiment, enabling them to adjust marketing strategies in real-time and maintain a competitive edge.

Case Study: Compact AI for Chatbot Development in Customer Support

Background:

A leading telecommunications company sought to improve its customer support experience by automating responses to customer queries through a chatbot. The goal was to develop an AI-powered solution that could provide 24/7 assistance, resolve common issues, and route more complex queries to human agents. However, the challenge was to deploy a **lightweight chatbot model** capable of running on edge devices and low-latency cloud services without sacrificing accuracy.

To meet this requirement, the company decided to use a **small language model**, specifically **DistilBERT**, for building the chatbot's natural language understanding (NLU) capabilities. The small model was selected to ensure quick response times and reduce resource consumption, while still being able to process a wide range of customer inquiries.

Solution Approach:

The project was broken down into several phases:

1. **Data Collection**: A dataset of common customer queries was collected, including questions related to account management, billing, and service requests.
2. **Model Selection**: **DistilBERT**, a compact variant of the BERT model, was selected for its balance between model size and accuracy.
3. **Fine-Tuning**: DistilBERT was fine-tuned on the collected dataset to understand customer queries in the context of telecommunications.
4. **Deployment**: The fine-tuned model was deployed

in a chatbot service that could handle common customer inquiries with real-time responses.

Implementation Details

1. Install Required Libraries

```
pip install transformers torch
```

2. Data Preprocessing

The dataset consists of common customer questions and corresponding intents. In this example, we'll assume a simple dataset with questions related to account management, service status, and billing.

```
import pandas as pd
from sklearn.model_selection import train_test_split
from transformers import DistilBertTokenizer

# Example dataset with customer queries and intents
data = {
    'query': ['How do I check my balance?', 'What is my bill for this month?', 'Is my internet working?',
              'How can I upgrade my plan?', 'Why is my account suspended?', 'Can I change my payment method?'],
    'intent': ['Balance Inquiry', 'Billing Inquiry', 'Service Status', 'Plan Upgrade', 'Account Issues', 'Payment Method']
}

df = pd.DataFrame(data)

# Split dataset into training and testing
train_data, test_data = train_test_split(df, test_size=0.2)

# Initialize the DistilBERT tokenizer
```

```
tokenizer = DistilBertTokenizer.from_pretrained('distilbert-base-uncased')

# Preprocess the queries using the tokenizer
def preprocess_data(texts, tokenizer, max_length=128):
    return tokenizer(texts, padding=True, truncation=True, max_length=max_length)

# Process the training and testing data
train_encodings = preprocess_data(train_data['query'].tolist(), tokenizer)
test_encodings = preprocess_data(test_data['query'].tolist(), tokenizer)

# Convert intents to integer labels
intent_map = {intent: idx for idx, intent in enumerate(df['intent'].unique())}
train_labels = train_data['intent'].map(intent_map).tolist()
test_labels = test_data['intent'].map(intent_map).tolist()
```

3. Model Fine-Tuning

The **DistilBERT** model will be fine-tuned for intent classification.

```
from transformers import DistilBertForSequenceClassification, Trainer, TrainingArguments
import torch

# Define a custom dataset class for PyTorch
class QueryDataset(torch.utils.data.Dataset):
    def __init__(self, encodings, labels):
```

```
        self.encodings = encodings
        self.labels = labels

    def __getitem__(self, idx):
        item = {key: torch.tensor(val[idx]) for key, val in
self.encodings.items()}
        item['labels'] = torch.tensor(self.labels[idx])
        return item

    def __len__(self):
        return len(self.labels)

# Create datasets for training and testing
train_dataset = QueryDataset(train_encodings, train_labels)
test_dataset = QueryDataset(test_encodings, test_labels)

# Load DistilBERT for sequence classification (6 intents in this
case)
model =
DistilBertForSequenceClassification.from_pretrained('distilbe
rt-base-uncased', num_labels=len(intent_map))

# Set up training arguments
training_args = TrainingArguments(
    output_dir='./results',
    num_train_epochs=3,
    per_device_train_batch_size=16,
    per_device_eval_batch_size=64,
    warmup_steps=500,
```

```
    weight_decay=0.01,
    logging_dir='./logs',
    logging_steps=10,
)

# Initialize Trainer
trainer = Trainer(
    model=model,
    args=training_args,
    train_dataset=train_dataset,
    eval_dataset=test_dataset,
)

# Fine-tune the model
trainer.train()
```

4. Model Evaluation

Once training is complete, we evaluate the model to check its performance.

```
# Evaluate the model on the test dataset
trainer.evaluate()
```

5. Real-Time Intent Prediction

The model can now be used to predict the intent of new customer queries in real time.

```
# Function to predict the intent of a new customer query
def predict_intent(query, model, tokenizer):
    inputs = tokenizer(query, return_tensors="pt", truncation=True, padding=True, max_length=128)
    outputs = model(inputs)
```

```
    logits = outputs.logits
    prediction = torch.argmax(logits, dim=1).item()
    return list(intent_map.keys())[prediction]

# Test with a sample query
new_query = "Can I change my payment method?"
predicted_intent = predict_intent(new_query, model, tokenizer)
print(f"Predicted Intent: {predicted_intent}")
```

6. Optimizing for Deployment

To deploy the model on edge devices or in low-cost cloud instances, the model can be converted to **ONNX** format for faster inference.

```
import torch.onnx

# Convert the trained model to ONNX format
onnx_path = 'chatbot_intent_model.onnx'
dummy_input = torch.ones(1, 128, dtype=torch.long)  # 1 example, 128 tokens

# Export the model to ONNX
torch.onnx.export(model, dummy_input, onnx_path, export_params=True, opset_version=12)
```

Key Results and Impact

- **Real-Time Customer Support**: The chatbot is able to classify customer queries in real-time and provide automated responses or route requests to the appropriate human agent.
- **Resource Efficiency**: By using a small model like **DistilBERT**, the company achieved fast inference

speeds while keeping resource consumption low, making the solution scalable for high-volume customer interactions.

- **Accuracy**: The model successfully identifies the intent of customer queries, even when they are worded differently, enabling the chatbot to provide accurate responses for a wide range of inquiries.
- **Scalability**: The model is lightweight enough to be deployed on cloud services with minimal computational overhead or even on edge devices in remote locations, where latency is critical.

Conclusion

This case study illustrates how **small language models** like **DistilBERT** can be used in practical applications like building intelligent chatbots for customer support. By leveraging compact models, companies can provide efficient, accurate, and scalable solutions without the need for heavy computational resources. This approach also ensures that the chatbot can operate in real-time, delivering an enhanced customer experience while maintaining cost-effectiveness.

Case Study: Small Language Models for Sentiment Analysis in E-Commerce

Background:

An e-commerce platform needed to enhance customer experience by analyzing customer reviews and feedback for sentiment analysis. The goal was to automatically categorize reviews as **positive**, **negative**, or **neutral** in real time to gain insights into customer satisfaction and make data-driven decisions regarding product improvements, customer service, and marketing.

The company faced the following challenges:

- **Scalability**: The platform generates a large volume of

reviews daily, and the solution needed to handle this influx in real-time.

- **Accuracy and Responsiveness**: The sentiment analysis model needed to perform well in identifying subtle sentiments in text, including sarcasm, while maintaining low latency.
- **Resource Efficiency**: The company wanted the solution to be lightweight and run on edge devices or low-cost cloud instances to reduce operational costs.

Given these requirements, the company decided to explore the use of **small language models** like **DistilBERT** for the sentiment analysis task.

Solution Approach:

The company decided to use **DistilBERT**, a distilled version of the popular BERT model, to fine-tune it for sentiment analysis on customer reviews. DistilBERT is a compact model that offers a good trade-off between accuracy and resource usage, making it an ideal choice for the platform's needs.

Steps Taken:

1. **Data Collection**: A dataset of customer reviews labeled with sentiment categories (positive, negative, neutral) was collected.
2. **Preprocessing**: Text data was cleaned and tokenized for use with the DistilBERT model.
3. **Fine-Tuning**: The pre-trained DistilBERT model was fine-tuned on the sentiment-labeled dataset.
4. **Deployment**: The fine-tuned model was deployed in a production environment for real-time sentiment classification of incoming reviews.

Implementation Details

1. Install Required Libraries

pip install transformers datasets torch

2. Data Preprocessing

For the purpose of this case study, let's assume the dataset is in CSV format with columns review_text (the text of the review) and sentiment (the sentiment label: 0 = Negative, 1 = Positive, 2 = Neutral).

```
import pandas as pd

from sklearn.model_selection import train_test_split

from transformers import DistilBertTokenizer


# Load the dataset

data = pd.read_csv('customer_reviews.csv')


# Split dataset into training and testing

train_data, test_data = train_test_split(data, test_size=0.2)


# Initialize the tokenizer for DistilBERT

tokenizer = DistilBertTokenizer.from_pretrained('distilbert-base-uncased')


# Preprocessing function

def preprocess_data(texts, tokenizer, max_length=128):

    return tokenizer(texts, padding=True, truncation=True, max_length=max_length)


# Preprocess the training and test texts

train_encodings = preprocess_data(train_data['review_text'].tolist(), tokenizer)

test_encodings = preprocess_data(test_data['review_text'].tolist(), tokenizer)
```

```
# Convert labels to integers
train_labels = train_data['sentiment'].tolist()
test_labels = test_data['sentiment'].tolist()
```

3. Model Training

The model is fine-tuned using the **DistilBERT** architecture for sentiment classification.

```
from transformers import DistilBertForSequenceClassification, Trainer, TrainingArguments
import torch

# Define a custom dataset class for PyTorch
class ReviewsDataset(torch.utils.data.Dataset):
    def __init__(self, encodings, labels):
        self.encodings = encodings
        self.labels = labels

    def __getitem__(self, idx):
        item = {key: torch.tensor(val[idx]) for key, val in self.encodings.items()}
        item['labels'] = torch.tensor(self.labels[idx])
        return item

    def __len__(self):
        return len(self.labels)

# Create the datasets for training and testing
train_dataset = ReviewsDataset(train_encodings, train_labels)
```

```
test_dataset = ReviewsDataset(test_encodings, test_labels)

# Load DistilBERT for sequence classification
model =
DistilBertForSequenceClassification.from_pretrained('distilbe
rt-base-uncased', num_labels=3)

# Set up training arguments
training_args = TrainingArguments(
    output_dir='./results',
    num_train_epochs=3,
    per_device_train_batch_size=16,
    per_device_eval_batch_size=64,
    warmup_steps=500,
    weight_decay=0.01,
    logging_dir='./logs',
    logging_steps=10,
)

# Initialize Trainer
trainer = Trainer(
    model=model,
    args=training_args,
    train_dataset=train_dataset,
    eval_dataset=test_dataset,
)

# Train the model
```

```
trainer.train()
```

4. Model Evaluation

Once training is complete, the model is evaluated on the test dataset.

```
# Evaluate the model on the test dataset
trainer.evaluate()
```

5. Real-Time Sentiment Prediction

The trained model can now be used for real-time sentiment analysis of new customer reviews.

```
# Function to predict sentiment of a new review
def predict_sentiment(review, model, tokenizer):
    inputs = tokenizer(review, return_tensors="pt", truncation=True, padding=True, max_length=128)
    outputs = model(inputs)
    logits = outputs.logits
    prediction = torch.argmax(logits, dim=1).item()
    sentiment_dict = {0: "Negative", 1: "Positive", 2: "Neutral"}
    return sentiment_dict[prediction]

# Test with a sample review
new_review = "This product is absolutely amazing! I love it."
prediction = predict_sentiment(new_review, model, tokenizer)
print(f"Sentiment: {prediction}")
```

6. Model Optimization for Deployment

For production use, the model can be exported to **ONNX** format to speed up inference, especially on edge devices.

```
import torch.onnx
```

```
# Convert the trained model to ONNX format
onnx_path = 'sentiment_analysis_model.onnx'
dummy_input = torch.ones(1, 128, dtype=torch.long) # 1 example, 128 tokens

# Export the model to ONNX
torch.onnx.export(model, dummy_input, onnx_path, export_params=True, opset_version=12)
```

Key Results and Impact

- **Real-Time Sentiment Analysis**: The sentiment analysis system now processes reviews in real-time, enabling the e-commerce platform to gain immediate insights into customer feedback.
- **Scalable**: The solution can handle thousands of incoming reviews per day with low-latency responses, even under heavy traffic conditions.
- **Efficient**: DistilBERT, being a smaller model, allows for fast inference on resource-constrained environments like mobile devices and low-cost cloud instances.
- **Accurate**: The model achieved high accuracy in classifying customer reviews as positive, negative, or neutral, even handling complex sentence structures and nuances like sarcasm.

Conclusion

This case study demonstrates how **small language models** like **DistilBERT** can be applied effectively in real-time sentiment analysis for large-scale e-commerce platforms. By leveraging a compact model, the company was able to provide accurate sentiment insights without the high computational overhead, enabling faster response times and lower operational costs.

The solution helps the company continuously improve customer experience based on real-time feedback while scaling to handle a large volume of reviews.

Case Study: Small Language Models for Automated Content Moderation in Online Communities

Background:

An online community platform hosts user-generated content, including comments, reviews, and discussions. The platform needed to implement an automated content moderation system to identify inappropriate, offensive, or harmful content in real-time, ensuring a safe environment for users.

The company faced several challenges:

- **Scalability**: The platform receives thousands of new posts and comments per day.
- **Efficiency**: It needed a solution that could run efficiently on low-resource environments without compromising response times.
- **Accuracy**: The model had to be accurate enough to identify offensive language, hate speech, and other undesirable content.

Given these challenges, the company chose to explore the potential of **small language models** that could perform content moderation tasks efficiently while being easy to deploy on edge devices (like mobile phones) and back-end systems.

Solution Approach:

The company decided to use a **distilled version of BERT (DistilBERT)** for the task of content moderation. DistilBERT is a smaller version of BERT that retains much of the original model's performance but with fewer parameters, making it an ideal choice for real-time text classification tasks.

The project involved the following steps:

1. **Data Collection**: A dataset of labeled comments containing toxic, offensive, or harmful content was gathered.
2. **Preprocessing**: The text data was cleaned, tokenized, and formatted for input into the DistilBERT model.
3. **Model Training**: The team fine-tuned a pre-trained **DistilBERT** model on the dataset of toxic comments.
4. **Real-Time Deployment**: The fine-tuned model was converted to an **ONNX format** to enable real-time inference on multiple platforms.

Implementation Details

1. Install Required Libraries

Before starting, install the necessary libraries:

```
pip install transformers datasets torch onnx
```

2. Data Preprocessing

The team loaded a publicly available dataset of toxic comments and preprocessed it for use with the model.

```
import pandas as pd

from sklearn.model_selection import train_test_split

from transformers import DistilBertTokenizer


# Load dataset (assumed CSV with 'comment' and 'label' columns, 1=toxic, 0=non-toxic)

comments_data = pd.read_csv('comments_data.csv')


# Split data into training and validation sets

train_data, val_data = train_test_split(comments_data, test_size=0.2)
```

```
# Initialize tokenizer for DistilBERT
tokenizer = DistilBertTokenizer.from_pretrained('distilbert-base-uncased')

# Preprocessing function
def preprocess_data(texts, tokenizer, max_length=128):
    return tokenizer(texts, padding=True, truncation=True, max_length=max_length)

# Preprocess the training and validation texts
train_texts = train_data['comment'].tolist()
val_texts = val_data['comment'].tolist()

train_encodings = preprocess_data(train_texts, tokenizer)
val_encodings = preprocess_data(val_texts, tokenizer)
```

3. Model Training

Next, the team fine-tuned **DistilBERT** for binary classification (toxic vs. non-toxic).

```
from transformers import DistilBertForSequenceClassification, Trainer, TrainingArguments
import torch

# Convert labels to integers (0=non-toxic, 1=toxic)
train_labels = train_data['label'].tolist()
val_labels = val_data['label'].tolist()

# Define a custom dataset class for PyTorch
class CommentsDataset(torch.utils.data.Dataset):
```

```
    def __init__(self, encodings, labels):
        self.encodings = encodings
        self.labels = labels

    def __getitem__(self, idx):
        item = {key: torch.tensor(val[idx]) for key, val in self.encodings.items()}
        item['labels'] = torch.tensor(self.labels[idx])
        return item

    def __len__(self):
        return len(self.labels)

# Create the train and validation datasets
train_dataset = CommentsDataset(train_encodings, train_labels)
val_dataset = CommentsDataset(val_encodings, val_labels)

# Load DistilBERT for sequence classification
model = DistilBertForSequenceClassification.from_pretrained('distilbert-base-uncased', num_labels=2)

# Define training arguments
training_args = TrainingArguments(
    output_dir='./results',
    num_train_epochs=3,
    per_device_train_batch_size=16,
    per_device_eval_batch_size=64,
```

```
    warmup_steps=500,
    weight_decay=0.01,
    logging_dir='./logs',
    logging_steps=10,
)

# Initialize Trainer
trainer = Trainer(
    model=model,
    args=training_args,
    train_dataset=train_dataset,
    eval_dataset=val_dataset,
)

# Train the model
trainer.train()
```

4. Model Evaluation

Once training is complete, evaluate the model on the validation dataset.

```
# Evaluate the model on the validation set
trainer.evaluate()
```

5. Real-Time Content Moderation

After fine-tuning, the model can be used for real-time content moderation. Here's how the model predicts whether a comment is toxic or non-toxic.

```
# Function to predict toxicity of a new comment
def predict_toxicity(comment, model, tokenizer):
    inputs = tokenizer(comment, return_tensors="pt",
```

```
truncation=True, padding=True, max_length=128)
    outputs = model(inputs)
    logits = outputs.logits
    prediction = torch.argmax(logits, dim=1).item()
    return "Toxic" if prediction == 1 else "Non-Toxic"

# Test with a sample comment
new_comment = "You are terrible and should be banned!"
prediction = predict_toxicity(new_comment, model, tokenizer)
print(f"Prediction: {prediction}")
```

6. Model Optimization for Deployment

To deploy the model in production, it was converted into **ONNX** format for fast inference on different devices.

```
import onnx
import torch.onnx

# Convert the trained model to ONNX format
onnx_path = 'content_moderation_model.onnx'
dummy_input = torch.ones(1, 128, dtype=torch.long)  # 1 example, 128 tokens

# Export the model to ONNX format
torch.onnx.export(model, dummy_input, onnx_path, export_params=True, opset_version=12)
```

Key Results and Impact

- **Real-Time Moderation**: The content moderation system now flags inappropriate comments in real-time, significantly reducing manual moderation efforts.

- **Efficient and Scalable**: The use of **DistilBERT**, a smaller version of BERT, ensures the model runs efficiently on both server-side systems and edge devices, even with large volumes of incoming content.
- **Accuracy**: The model achieved a high level of accuracy in identifying toxic comments while maintaining speed and scalability.
- **Improved User Experience**: By automatically detecting and removing harmful content, the platform provides a safer and more positive environment for its users.

Conclusion

This case study demonstrates the power of **small language models** like **DistilBERT** for real-time, automated content moderation in online communities. By leveraging a compact model, the company was able to balance accuracy with efficiency, making it suitable for deployment in production environments with limited computational resources. The solution not only addressed the company's needs for scalable, real-time moderation but also enhanced the overall user experience by ensuring a safe, respectful space for online interactions.

Case Study: Compact AI for Sentiment Analysis in Customer Feedback

Background:

A retail company receives a significant amount of customer feedback through surveys, emails, and social media. The feedback is diverse, with both positive and negative sentiments expressed. The company wanted to automate the analysis of customer sentiment to quickly identify customer satisfaction trends and address potential issues.

Given the need for a lightweight and efficient solution, the company decided to explore **small language models** that could run on their internal systems without requiring substantial computational resources. The solution needed to accurately classify customer feedback as **positive**, **neutral**, or **negative** and be capable of real-time analysis.

Solution Approach:

The company selected a compact AI model, **TinyBERT**, which is a smaller version of the popular BERT model, optimized for sentiment analysis. The goal was to fine-tune **TinyBERT** to classify customer feedback and deploy it as a real-time system capable of analyzing incoming feedback instantly.

Steps:

1. **Data Collection**: The company collected historical customer feedback, including product reviews, survey responses, and social media mentions, labeled with sentiment labels (positive, neutral, negative).
2. **Preprocessing**: The text data was cleaned, tokenized, and prepared for input into the **TinyBERT** model.
3. **Model Selection and Training**: The team chose **TinyBERT** for sentiment classification due to its efficiency in terms of both size and performance.
4. **Model Optimization and Deployment**: The model was optimized for deployment in real-time using **ONNX** (Open Neural Network Exchange) format, ensuring it could be deployed on different systems and devices.

Implementation Details

1. Install Required Libraries

We begin by installing the necessary libraries:

```
pip install transformers datasets torch onnx
```

2. Data Preprocessing

Next, we preprocess the customer feedback data and tokenize it for **TinyBERT**.

```
import pandas as pd
from datasets import load_dataset
from sklearn.model_selection import train_test_split
from transformers import TinyBertTokenizer

# Load dataset (assuming a CSV file with 'feedback' and 'sentiment' columns)
customer_feedback = pd.read_csv('customer_feedback.csv')

# Split data into train and validation sets
train_data, val_data = train_test_split(customer_feedback, test_size=0.2)

# Tokenizer for TinyBERT
tokenizer = TinyBertTokenizer.from_pretrained('huawei-noah/TinyBERT_General_4L_312D')

# Function to preprocess and tokenize the feedback
def preprocess_data(texts, tokenizer, max_length=128):
    return tokenizer(texts, padding=True, truncation=True, max_length=max_length)

# Preprocess the train and validation data
train_texts = train_data['feedback'].tolist()
val_texts = val_data['feedback'].tolist()
```

```
train_encodings = preprocess_data(train_texts, tokenizer)
val_encodings = preprocess_data(val_texts, tokenizer)
```

3. Model Training

We will fine-tune the **TinyBERT** model for sentiment classification (positive, neutral, and negative).

```
from transformers import TinyBertForSequenceClassification, Trainer, TrainingArguments
import torch

# Convert labels to integers (0=negative, 1=neutral, 2=positive)
train_labels = train_data['sentiment'].tolist()
val_labels = val_data['sentiment'].tolist()

# Create PyTorch datasets
class FeedbackDataset(torch.utils.data.Dataset):
    def __init__(self, encodings, labels):
        self.encodings = encodings
        self.labels = labels

    def __getitem__(self, idx):
        item = {key: torch.tensor(val[idx]) for key, val in self.encodings.items()}
        item['labels'] = torch.tensor(self.labels[idx])
        return item

    def __len__(self):
        return len(self.labels)
```

```
# Create train and validation datasets
train_dataset = FeedbackDataset(train_encodings, train_labels)
val_dataset = FeedbackDataset(val_encodings, val_labels)

# Load TinyBERT for sequence classification
model = TinyBertForSequenceClassification.from_pretrained('huawei-noah/TinyBERT_General_4L_312D', num_labels=3)

# Define training arguments
training_args = TrainingArguments(
    output_dir='./results',
    num_train_epochs=3,
    per_device_train_batch_size=16,
    per_device_eval_batch_size=64,
    warmup_steps=500,
    weight_decay=0.01,
    logging_dir='./logs',
    logging_steps=10,
)

# Initialize Trainer
trainer = Trainer(
    model=model,
    args=training_args,
    train_dataset=train_dataset,
    eval_dataset=val_dataset,
```

```
)

# Train the model
trainer.train()
```

4. Model Evaluation

After training, we evaluate the model's performance on the validation dataset.

```
# Evaluate the model on the validation dataset
trainer.evaluate()
```

5. Real-Time Sentiment Classification

Once trained, the model is ready to be used for real-time sentiment classification of new customer feedback.

```
# Function to predict sentiment of customer feedback
def predict_sentiment(feedback, model, tokenizer):
    inputs = tokenizer(feedback, return_tensors="pt", truncation=True, padding=True, max_length=128)
    outputs = model(inputs)
    logits = outputs.logits
    prediction = torch.argmax(logits, dim=1).item()
    if prediction == 0:
        return "Negative"
    elif prediction == 1:
        return "Neutral"
    else:
        return "Positive"

# Test with a sample feedback
new_feedback = "I absolutely love this product! It's amazing."
```

```
prediction = predict_sentiment(new_feedback, model, tokenizer)

print(f"Sentiment: {prediction}")
```

6. Model Optimization for Deployment

The trained model is then converted to **ONNX** format for real-time deployment across various platforms.

```
import onnx

from transformers import TinyBertForSequenceClassification


# Save the model as a PyTorch model first

model.save_pretrained("sentiment_model")


# Convert to ONNX

import torch.onnx


# Dummy input for model conversion

dummy_input = torch.ones(1, 128, dtype=torch.long) # 1 example, 128 tokens

onnx_path = 'sentiment_model.onnx'


# Convert to ONNX format

torch.onnx.export(model, dummy_input, onnx_path, export_params=True, opset_version=12)
```

Key Results and Impact

- **Real-Time Sentiment Analysis**: The company can now classify customer feedback in real-time, enabling quick responses to both positive and negative sentiments.
- **Compact Model for Mobile Devices**: The compact **TinyBERT** model runs efficiently on mobile devices

and embedded systems, ensuring fast feedback processing without high computational costs.

- **Scalable**: The model can handle large volumes of incoming feedback, making it scalable to meet the demands of a global customer base.
- **Customer Experience Improvement**: By quickly identifying and addressing negative feedback, the company can improve customer satisfaction and loyalty.

Conclusion

This case study highlights how **small language models** like **TinyBERT** can be applied effectively for **sentiment analysis** in a business context. The company achieved significant improvements in customer feedback analysis by using a compact model that operates efficiently on low-resource devices while maintaining high accuracy. This approach offers a blueprint for other companies looking to implement AI-driven solutions in real-time applications without compromising on performance or resource consumption.

CASE STUDY: COMPACT AI FOR REAL-TIME SPAM DETECTION IN EMAILS

Background:

A leading email service provider wanted to enhance its spam filtering system. The goal was to improve the accuracy of spam detection while ensuring the solution was lightweight and could run efficiently on mobile devices and low-resource environments. The company had already been using traditional machine learning methods, but these models were slow and required significant computational power. Therefore, the company needed a **compact AI model** that could classify emails as spam or not-spam in real-time, even in resource-constrained environments.

Solution Approach:

The company decided to use **small language models**, specifically a fine-tuned version of **DistilBERT**, to perform the spam classification. The main advantage of using a small transformer model like **DistilBERT** is that it provides excellent classification accuracy while being more efficient in terms of both computational resources and latency.

Steps:

1. **Dataset Collection**: The company collected a labeled dataset of emails containing spam and non-spam examples.
2. **Preprocessing**: The dataset was cleaned and tokenized for input into the language model.
3. **Model Selection and Training**: The team fine-tuned a pre-trained **DistilBERT** model to classify emails as spam or not-spam.
4. **Deployment**: The trained model was optimized for real-time use on edge devices using **TensorFlow Lite** for low-latency and efficient spam detection.

Implementation Details

1. Installing Required Libraries

First, install the necessary libraries:

```
pip install transformers datasets torch tensorflow
```

2. Data Preprocessing

For simplicity, let's assume the dataset is already labeled with spam (1) and non-spam (0) labels. Here's how we can preprocess the data and tokenize it for the model.

```
import pandas as pd
from datasets import load_dataset
from sklearn.model_selection import train_test_split
from transformers import DistilBertTokenizer

# Load dataset (assuming a simple CSV with "text" and "label" columns)
email_data = pd.read_csv('spam_dataset.csv')

# Split the data into training and validation sets
```

```
train_data, val_data = train_test_split(email_data, test_size=0.2)

# Tokenizer for DistilBERT
tokenizer = DistilBertTokenizer.from_pretrained('distilbert-base-uncased')

# Function to preprocess and tokenize the data
def preprocess_data(texts, tokenizer, max_length=128):
    return tokenizer(texts, padding=True, truncation=True, max_length=max_length)

# Preprocess the train and validation data
train_texts = train_data['text'].tolist()
val_texts = val_data['text'].tolist()

train_encodings = preprocess_data(train_texts, tokenizer)
val_encodings = preprocess_data(val_texts, tokenizer)
```

3. Model Training

Now, we'll fine-tune the **DistilBERT** model to classify the emails as spam or not-spam.

```
from transformers import DistilBertForSequenceClassification, Trainer, TrainingArguments
import torch

# Convert labels to integers
train_labels = train_data['label'].tolist()
val_labels = val_data['label'].tolist()
```

```
# Create PyTorch datasets
class EmailDataset(torch.utils.data.Dataset):
    def __init__(self, encodings, labels):
        self.encodings = encodings
        self.labels = labels

    def __getitem__(self, idx):
        item = {key: torch.tensor(val[idx]) for key, val in
self.encodings.items()}
        item['labels'] = torch.tensor(self.labels[idx])
        return item

    def __len__(self):
        return len(self.labels)

# Create train and validation datasets
train_dataset = EmailDataset(train_encodings, train_labels)
val_dataset = EmailDataset(val_encodings, val_labels)

# Load the DistilBERT model for binary classification (spam vs.
non-spam)
model =
DistilBertForSequenceClassification.from_pretrained('distilbe
rt-base-uncased', num_labels=2)

# Define training arguments
training_args = TrainingArguments(
    output_dir='./results',          # Output directory for model
checkpoints
```

```
    num_train_epochs=3,
    per_device_train_batch_size=16,
    per_device_eval_batch_size=64,
    warmup_steps=500,
    weight_decay=0.01,
    logging_dir='./logs',        # Directory for storing logs
    logging_steps=10,
)

# Initialize the Trainer
trainer = Trainer(
    model=model,
    args=training_args,
    train_dataset=train_dataset,
    eval_dataset=val_dataset,
)

# Train the model
trainer.train()
```

4. Model Evaluation

After training, evaluate the model on the validation set to check its performance.

```
# Evaluate the model on the validation dataset
trainer.evaluate()
```

5. Real-Time Spam Detection for New Emails

Once the model is fine-tuned, it can be used for real-time spam detection on new incoming emails.

```
# Function to predict spam or not-spam for a given email
```

```
def predict_spam(email, model, tokenizer):
    inputs = tokenizer(email, return_tensors="pt", truncation=True, padding=True, max_length=128)
    outputs = model(inputs)
    logits = outputs.logits
    prediction = torch.argmax(logits, dim=1).item()
    return "spam" if prediction == 1 else "not spam"

# Test the model with a new email
new_email = "Congratulations! You've won a free gift card. Click here to claim it."
prediction = predict_spam(new_email, model, tokenizer)
print(f"Prediction: {prediction}")
```

6. Deployment for Real-Time Use

For real-time deployment on mobile devices or low-resource environments, the model needs to be optimized for efficiency. This can be done by converting the trained model to **TensorFlow Lite** format for fast inference.

```
import tensorflow as tf

# Convert the PyTorch model to TensorFlow format
model.save_pretrained('saved_model')

# Load the model in TensorFlow
model = tf.saved_model.load('saved_model')

# Convert the model to TensorFlow Lite format
converter = tf.lite.TFLiteConverter.from_saved_model('saved_model')
```

```
tflite_model = converter.convert()

# Save the converted TensorFlow Lite model
with open('spam_detection_model.tflite', 'wb') as f:
    f.write(tflite_model)
```

Key Results and Impact

- **Real-Time Spam Detection**: The compact AI model provides real-time spam classification with minimal latency, making it ideal for integration into email systems.
- **Efficient Resource Usage**: By using a smaller model like **DistilBERT**, the solution is computationally efficient and can run on mobile devices or low-resource environments, without compromising performance.
- **Scalability**: The model can easily scale to handle millions of emails per day while maintaining accuracy and speed, even in cloud environments or on edge devices.
- **Improved User Experience**: By automatically filtering out spam in real-time, the solution enhances the user experience by ensuring only relevant emails are visible to the user.

Conclusion

This case study demonstrates how **small language models** can be applied to a critical task like **spam detection** in emails. By using a compact transformer model like **DistilBERT**, the company was able to build a lightweight and efficient solution for real-time email classification, significantly improving the user experience while ensuring that the model could run on devices with limited resources. This use case highlights the power and versatility of small AI models in solving practical problems while maintaining high efficiency.

CASE STUDY: COMPACT AI FOR REAL-TIME SENTIMENT ANALYSIS IN CUSTOMER FEEDBACK

Background:

A global e-commerce company receives thousands of customer feedback responses daily, ranging from product reviews to post-purchase surveys. Analyzing this feedback manually is labor-intensive and time-consuming. The company needs an automated solution that can quickly identify the sentiment of customer feedback (positive, neutral, or negative) and provide insights to improve customer satisfaction. Since the company operates in a variety of regions with different languages, they need a solution that can handle multiple languages efficiently without requiring extensive computational resources.

The solution must be built using **compact AI models** that can run on the company's existing infrastructure, which includes cloud-based systems as well as edge devices for real-time feedback processing.

Solution Approach:

The company decides to use a **small language model** for **real-time sentiment analysis**. A lightweight model like **DistilBERT** (a smaller version of BERT) is ideal because it offers a good balance between performance and resource efficiency. The solution will process customer feedback in multiple languages and classify the sentiment as positive, neutral, or negative. Additionally, the model will be optimized for real-time processing using **ONNX** or **TensorFlow Lite**.

Steps:

1. **Dataset Collection**: Collect a labeled dataset of customer feedback with sentiments (positive, negative, neutral).
2. **Preprocessing**: Preprocess the dataset and tokenize the text for training.
3. **Model Selection and Training**: Fine-tune a small transformer-based model like **DistilBERT** for sentiment analysis.
4. **Deployment**: Optimize and deploy the trained model for real-time sentiment analysis on customer feedback.

Implementation Details

1. Installing Required Libraries

First, install the required libraries:

pip install transformers datasets torch sklearn

2. Data Preprocessing

For this case, we'll use a sample dataset of customer feedback with sentiment labels and preprocess it for training.

from datasets import load_dataset

from transformers import DistilBertTokenizer

```
from sklearn.model_selection import train_test_split

# Sample dataset of customer feedback (for illustration purposes)
feedback_data = [
    {"text": "The product is amazing, I love it!", "sentiment": "positive"},
    {"text": "This is the worst purchase I've ever made.", "sentiment": "negative"},
    {"text": "It was okay, nothing special.", "sentiment": "neutral"},
    {"text": "Excellent customer service, very helpful!", "sentiment": "positive"},
    {"text": "The item was broken when it arrived.", "sentiment": "negative"},
    {"text": "Good quality, but the shipping was delayed.", "sentiment": "neutral"}
]

# Convert the dataset into a format suitable for training
df = pd.DataFrame(feedback_data)

# Split the data into training and validation sets
train_data, val_data = train_test_split(df, test_size=0.2)

# Tokenizer for DistilBERT
tokenizer = DistilBertTokenizer.from_pretrained('distilbert-base-uncased')

# Function to preprocess and tokenize the data
```

```
def preprocess_data(texts, tokenizer, max_length=128):
    return tokenizer(texts, padding=True, truncation=True, max_length=max_length)

# Preprocess the train and validation data
train_texts = train_data['text'].tolist()
val_texts = val_data['text'].tolist()

train_encodings = preprocess_data(train_texts, tokenizer)
val_encodings = preprocess_data(val_texts, tokenizer)
```

3. Model Training

We will fine-tune **DistilBERT** for sentiment classification.

```
from transformers import DistilBertForSequenceClassification, Trainer, TrainingArguments
import torch

# Convert the sentiments to numerical labels (positive=0, neutral=1, negative=2)
sentiment_map = {"positive": 0, "neutral": 1, "negative": 2}
train_labels = train_data['sentiment'].map(sentiment_map).tolist()
val_labels = val_data['sentiment'].map(sentiment_map).tolist()

# Create PyTorch datasets
class FeedbackDataset(torch.utils.data.Dataset):
    def __init__(self, encodings, labels):
        self.encodings = encodings
```

```
        self.labels = labels

    def __getitem__(self, idx):
        item = {key: torch.tensor(val[idx]) for key, val in self.encodings.items()}
        item['labels'] = torch.tensor(self.labels[idx])
        return item

    def __len__(self):
        return len(self.labels)

# Create train and validation datasets
train_dataset = FeedbackDataset(train_encodings, train_labels)
val_dataset = FeedbackDataset(val_encodings, val_labels)

# Load the DistilBERT model for sequence classification
model = DistilBertForSequenceClassification.from_pretrained('distilbert-base-uncased', num_labels=3)

# Define training arguments
training_args = TrainingArguments(
    output_dir='./results',          # Output directory for model checkpoints
    num_train_epochs=3,
    per_device_train_batch_size=16,
    per_device_eval_batch_size=64,
    warmup_steps=500,
    weight_decay=0.01,
```

```
    logging_dir='./logs',         # Directory for storing logs
    logging_steps=10,
)

# Initialize the Trainer
trainer = Trainer(
    model=model,
    args=training_args,
    train_dataset=train_dataset,
    eval_dataset=val_dataset,
)

# Train the model
trainer.train()
```

4. Model Evaluation

Once the model is trained, evaluate its performance on the validation set.

```
# Evaluate the model on the validation dataset
trainer.evaluate()
```

5. Real-Time Sentiment Analysis for Customer Feedback

Once the model is fine-tuned, it can be used for real-time sentiment analysis of incoming customer feedback.

```
# Function to predict sentiment of a single feedback
def predict_sentiment(feedback, model, tokenizer):
    inputs = tokenizer(feedback, return_tensors="pt", truncation=True, padding=True, max_length=128)
    outputs = model(inputs)
    logits = outputs.logits
```

```
    prediction = torch.argmax(logits, dim=1).item()
    sentiment_map_reverse = {0: "positive", 1: "neutral", 2: "negative"}
    return sentiment_map_reverse[prediction]

# Test the model with new feedback
new_feedback = "I had a fantastic experience with the product!"
sentiment = predict_sentiment(new_feedback, model, tokenizer)
print(f"Sentiment: {sentiment}")
```

6. Deployment

For deployment, you can use **ONNX** or **TensorFlow Lite** to optimize the model for real-time sentiment analysis on edge devices.

```
# Install TensorFlow and TensorFlow Lite converter
pip install tensorflow

# Convert the trained model to TensorFlow format
import tensorflow as tf

# Convert from Hugging Face's model to TensorFlow format
tf_model = tf.saved_model.load('path_to_finetuned_model')

# Save the model in TensorFlow Lite format
converter = tf.lite.TFLiteConverter.from_saved_model('path_to_finetuned_model')
tflite_model = converter.convert()
```

```
# Save the converted model
with open('sentiment_analysis_model.tflite', 'wb') as f:
    f.write(tflite_model)
```

Key Results and Impact

- **Real-Time Sentiment Analysis**: The **compact AI model** efficiently classifies customer feedback in real-time as positive, neutral, or negative, allowing the company to respond swiftly to customer needs.
- **Resource Efficiency**: The model is optimized for speed and resource consumption, running effectively on cloud infrastructure and edge devices, providing insights without requiring powerful hardware.
- **Scalability**: The solution can easily scale to process feedback in multiple languages, thanks to the compact AI's versatility and ability to handle various sentiment classification tasks.
- **Improved Customer Experience**: By automating sentiment analysis, the company can quickly detect negative feedback and address customer concerns promptly, improving overall satisfaction.

Conclusion

This case study demonstrates the power of **small language models** like **DistilBERT** for real-time sentiment analysis in customer feedback. With the right combination of model compression and deployment strategies, the company can achieve efficient, scalable, and accurate sentiment classification, improving their ability to respond to customers and enhance satisfaction.

www.ingramcontent.com/pod-product-compliance
Lightning Source LLC
La Vergne TN
LVHW051427050326
832903LV00030BD/2954
* 9 7 9 8 3 0 0 8 0 9 9 4 2 *